LONGMANS' CURRICULUM REFORM

History betrayed?

D1500717

£1.50 net   30/- net

LONGMANS' CURRICULUM REFORM SERIES
General Editor: Professor Jack Wrigley
Professor of Education and Curriculum Research and Development Reading
University

History betrayed?

M. B. Booth
Head of History Department
Burnt Mill Comprehensive School, Harlow

LONGMANS

LONGMANS, GREEN AND CO LTD
London and Harlow
Associated companies, branches and representatives throughout the world

© *Longmans, Green and Co Ltd* 1969
First Published 1969

SBN 582 32346 0 *paper edition*
SBN 582 32347 9 *cased edition*

Printed in Great Britain by Neill and Co Ltd. Edinburgh

To my parents

Foreword

Between 1963 and 1967 a group of people at Southampton University came together to work on the inter-related subjects of curriculum reform and consequent examination and assessment. We were aware of the interesting work which had been carried out by the Nuffield Foundation in science and mathematics and wanted to attempt similar work in the humanities – particularly in English, history and geography. We felt that the problem in the humanities was perhaps more difficult than the corresponding one for science. Teaching methods had been given a new stimulus in science by the advent of new content. But in English, history and geography there was, in our opinion, an equal need for a revision of methods of teaching and yet no obvious stimulus to be derived from new content. We all felt that the present external examination system inhibited good teaching and were determined in our research to investigate the interaction of curriculum and examinations. We hoped to keep our feet on the ground by working in close contact with both teachers and children, and thought that before we experimented with anything revolutionary we ought to make an analysis of present practices. We knew that there was much of great value in the best of present day teaching and wanted to learn from that.

We set out gaily, confident in the belief that we could do better and more relevant research than most others had done in this field. We also planned right from the outset that the results of the work would be presented in book-form. The task of producing worthwhile research proved more difficult than we had expected. A thesis is one thing – an interesting book on the same topic is another. If we have succeeded in raising the level of our work then it is due to the supreme advantage of working as a team and being able to discuss common problems with each other.

History Betrayed? is one of the first-fruits of our common endeavour and the first book in this new series on curriculum reform. Martin Booth's talent and persistence, his association with an active research group, and his experience in planning a new teaching syllabus as head of the history department in a comprehensive school, have all contributed to making this a unique and interesting book. His findings in the realms of good history teaching are not entirely new. Enlightened teachers and trainers of teachers have been saying some of the things advocated by Martin Booth for many years. But the impressive feature of the book is the way good practice is described by the teachers themselves, and the way their pupils confirm their own belief in the value of what good teachers and enlightened educators have been saying.

It is good to have progressive teaching methods described again by the author, by the teachers on the job, and most of all, by the pupils. But I suspect that the practising teacher will find the account of actual syllabuses, of teaching situations and of available books even more useful.

The work on assessment and examination described in the book is original, useful and interesting. We began with the conviction that much that is wrong in present-day history teaching can be ascribed to bad practices engendered by the external examination system in its conventional form. We still so believe and the book provides convincing evidence on these matters. The research shows how it might be possible to examine in history in a more enlightened way. It is fair to say that the situation in England and Wales with regard to examinations is a more open one now than it has ever been. The C S E and G C E Examining Boards are experimenting with new methods and the Schools Council for Curriculum and Examination is concerned to promote experiments. The most obvious way to reform is perhaps through the Mode 3 procedure, that is an internal examination externally moderated, and pioneered by the C S E Boards; but as Martin Booth makes clear, there is still something to be said for using written external examinations of a conventional form. This book suggests interesting new ways of setting questions and of using more sensible marking procedures. It also provides evidence that these new enterprising methods can be at least as reliable as the time-honoured methods. I hope they might be adopted widely – they are certainly quite feasible for there is nothing particularly complicated about them.

The book should be of interest and use to all teachers of history, to students in colleges of education and in university departments of education, and to their teachers and lecturers. We hope and believe that it restates the case for good teaching in history, provides evidence about this from teachers and pupils, that it gives help in terms of teaching procedures and syllabuses, and that it suggests new and better ways of examining and assessing the results of this better teaching. Above all, we hope that by basing the work on the actual teaching in the schools we have kept our feet on the ground.

Contents

Acknowledgements

My first thanks must go to the headteachers and staff who welcomed me into their schools and were so generous with their time. Without their active cooperation this survey could never have been attempted. I am deeply grateful to them all.

The pupils, too, played a vital role. They cheerfully completed questionnaires, sat test papers and endured long interviews. Their good natured and thoughtful contributions made my task at once more pleasant and more worthwhile. To all of them, my sincere thanks.

I must, of course, make myself entirely responsible for the interpretations and conclusions made on the material gathered; but I am very conscious of the help I have had in various ways from a number of people. Professor Jack Wrigley gave constant advice, help and encouragement; Mr R. Douch and Mr F. Dwyer were generous with their help and constructive criticism; Mr R. Odel gave valuable technical assistance during the construction of the tests; Mrs P. Taylor helped with the heavier statistical work; Mrs C. Rendel coped with the typing of a difficult manuscript. With Mr F. Inglis, Mr D. Dyne and Mr F. H. Sparrow I had many stimulating discussions on the problems examined in this book; but a particular thank you is due to Mr Sparrow, a secondary school history teacher of many years experience. He undertook the onerous task of marking the research history tests a second time; he was tireless with his advice and encouragement. I greatly valued his support. The script was also read by Miss M. E. Bryant, Mrs H. M. Booth and Mrs Coward who gave valuable criticism. To all these people I offer my profound thanks.

Finally, I owe thanks to the Department of Education and Science for the grant which covered the research on which this book is based, and to the Director and staff of the Southampton Institute of Education who made available the facilities of the Institute.

of *Journal* by George Fox, and would appreciate any information that would enable us to do so.

The illustrations on page 175 are redrawn from *Introduction to British History*, © the Clarendon Press 1954, by kind permission of the publishers.

Introduction

Secondary school history, it might seem, is flourishing. Every year large numbers of pupils enter for the 'O' level and C S E history examinations; in many secondary schools, history sixths are increasing in size; university departments have ample applicants. To the outsider the situation appears healthy. However, not all history teachers share this optimism; and there has been of late a growing disquiet, a questioning of current practice and reconsideration of the criteria on which syllabuses are based.

Such reappraisal has been prompted partly by outside pressures. On a general level, the Department of Education and Science Curriculum Study Group has raised the whole question of syllabus; the new C S E examinations, the problems of assessment. More particularly, a number of recent books, articles and lectures on history teaching have sharply criticised the traditional 'Outlines of English History' course; and their tendency has been to argue in favour of 'studies in depth' and, for fourth and fifth year pupils, twentieth-century and world history.

Within the schools, too, there are increasing pressures which have led to this reconsideration of history teaching. The very numbers entering for 'O' level and C S E have caused many to question the purpose of the public examination. For it often seems that fourth and fifth year history turns into a dreary grind, the object of which is to enable pupils to accumulate sufficient data in order to obtain a certificate; and valued aims have to be jettisoned in favour of objectives which at the best seem trivial, at the worst a travesty of what education should be about. Pressure, too, can come from other departments in the school. History has never had a prominent place in the school timetable; today history teachers are finding that its position needs justification because of the demands for more teaching time from the scientists and linguists. Our utilitarian society has tended to treat the impractical discipline of history with mild contempt; there is a danger that this attitude may become more hostile.

It was this situation that encouraged the investigation into the problems of secondary school history teaching and assessment which forms the basis of this book. The investigation was based on the theory that effective research into the content and teaching of a subject had to start within the school, and that suggestions for reform of syllabus or assessment must be based on an analysis of the actual classroom rather than on theoretical considerations. This, it was felt, would give the enquiry an immediacy and relevance which previous investigations had often lacked – though little research has in fact been done into the problems of history teaching and learning.

Five grammar schools in the south of England were asked to take part in the scheme, and between November 1965 and July 1966 an empirical survey of their history courses was undertaken. It was hoped that by concentrating on the particular problems of history teaching and learning of a group of schools it would be possible to illustrate and emphasise general points about history syllabus content, teaching techniques and examination construction. This detailed recording of actual practice and the broader recommendations which arise should be of interest and use to all history teachers – especially perhaps to those who are about to undertake a mode 3 c s e syllabus.

The approach of the investigation was twofold. First, the senior history teachers were asked to fill in a detailed questionnaire and later to discuss their written answers. The intention was to determine the situations in which they teach, to compare their syllabuses and teaching methods and, if possible, to uncover the aims and assumptions (often unformulated) that underlie their teaching. Secondly, history was examined from the pupils' points of view. Here it was hoped not only to see the classroom situation from the children's angle but also to explore different ways of assessing the nature and extent of their understanding in history. Ideally, this part of the enquiry should have been based on pupils in their fifth year at secondary school but the pressures of the external examination are such that the schools were understandably reluctant to allow these pupils to take part. Consequently, the sample of 147 boys and girls (approximately thirty pupils from each school) was taken from the fourth year. A fairly wide range of ability was ensured by choosing forms or sets from different streams.

As a start the pupils were asked to complete questionnaires on the teaching and learning of history. Their written answers to these and the subsequent discussions gave some indication of their attitude to the subject. This provided a background for the more detailed probing through written tests and interview of their historical knowledge. Here it was hoped to identify the insights achieved, as distinct from those fragments of knowledge which are learned by heart purely for the purposes of assessment and subsequently relegated to a mental lumber room. The distinction is a fine one, for there is interaction between historical thinking and historical fact (the 'human activity' which is the stuff of history); thinking in history must arise from a foundation of factual information just as this factual information is given shape and meaning by such mental activity. The difficulty, therefore, is to identify these mental processes: how can one distinguish between an answer consisting merely of rote learning and one which contains individual judgement and opinion? The research tests tried to deal with this difficulty by presenting the pupils with problems in history to which there would be little likelihood of the children having stock answers. They aimed, in fact, at making the pupils think in their own way round historical material.

The tests, however, were not only intended to explore the kind of thinking in history of which intelligent secondary school pupils are capable; it was also hoped to show that such examinations (which make a radical break with the traditional 'O' level paper) can serve as reliable and valid attainment tests. In examinations of this nature, the stumbling block is the marking scheme. A system was drawn up which was applied to the completed tests by two markers separately; and the extent of their marking agreement was determined by calculating coefficients of correlation.

The enquiry was concluded by interviewing the pupils either singly or in pairs, sometimes for as long as three-quarters of an hour. Here it was possible to explore more fully the questionnaire and test answers. Against the background of what the teachers had said, what was seen when lessons were observed and the I Q scores of the pupils, the strands of the project were brought together and an attempt made to draw conclusions.

The spoken and written material which the enquiry produced, is lengthy and diffuse and it needed fairly rigid treatment to give it shape. Much of the evidence is of a predictable nature; and it should be stressed that the investigation has not yielded final answers to the many and complex questions which beset us as history teachers. What it has done is to examine old problems from a different angle, to illuminate afresh difficulties we all face and to suggest approaches based on practical situations.

The investigation is based on particular schools, particular pupils; and though the book moves easily from the particular to the general, the evidence and recommendations are given greater sharpness when set against a description of the five schools and their history departments. This is the purpose of chapter one. The rest of the book deals with the evidence under the three headings of syllabus (chapter 2), teaching techniques and objectives (chapter 3) and examinations and assessment (chapters 4 and 5). The chapters on syllabus, and methods and objectives look at the problems first through the teachers' eyes, secondly through the pupils'; in each case they conclude by considering the implications of the evidence. Those on examinations discuss the problems of assessment in history, and the results of the marking and analysis of the research history tests.

Such a layout inevitably involves overlap, for syllabus, teaching techniques, objectives and assessment form something of a unity which it is difficult to divide. In the final chapter, however, the history curriculum is viewed as a whole; for the discussion of the pupils' written and spoken answers to the research history tests brings together the problems which are treated separately in the earlier chapters. What these lose in subtlety they gain perhaps in clarity and usefulness of presentation; in the fifth chapter the complexity and essential cohesion of the history teaching situation emerges most clearly.

1 The schools and their history departments

Benborough grammar school is coeducational and situated on the outskirts of a small, busy market town. The catchment area is large and some of the pupils have long bus journeys from the outlying villages; out-of-school activities tend to suffer because of this – for example, there is at the moment no history club. Though the school traces its foundation back to the sixteenth-century – the names of the headmasters from 1569 can be seen on a board in the main passage – the twentieth century was the period of the school's growth. The present low brick building surrounded by pleasant playing fields was put up in 1927; by that time the school was controlled by the local authority. It has at present just under 600 boys and girls. To describe the school as 'happy' is not particularly helpful; yet there is a bright and cheerful purposefulness about the place that can be explained by this adjective. Such a view is partly explained by a preference for coeducation; but the healthy good looks of the country children, the attractive burr of their accents and the directness of their speech, the neatness of the blazers and the freshness of the dresses, the crowded, tidy noticeboards, all combine to give a favourable inpression. The more obvious manifestations of tradition seem to play little part, but in a very real sense the school seems to be part of the local community, clear as to what its purpose is and proud of its close links with the town whose name it bears.

Daymer grammar school is for girls, and is of much more recent foundation (1905). It is under the control of the L E A and housed in modern buildings opened in 1960. It has approximately 700 pupils. Though the town to which it is attached is little bigger than Benborough, the social environment differs considerably. The large and popular seaside resort of Sandforth is only a few miles away, and the sprawl of its suburbs joins with the fringes of the town in which the school is situated. Neat bungalows and 'semis' with prim gardens line the road which leads to the school; and though the sea can just be seen from the attractive grounds which surround the school one is in no doubt that the overpopulated south of England is close at hand. Was it the suburban surroundings, then, and the fresh, modern building which gave an air of greater sophistication to these pupils? The girls did seem to have a certain poise and confidence; and the elegant hairstyles and nylons gave them a maturity which their years belied. Again, tradition seems to play little part in the life of the school – as the senior history mistress pointed out:

'I think it's more likely to happen with boys' schools than girls'; but

1

because the town to which is it attached is less tightly knit than Benborough and the suburban growth has blurred boundaries, the school seemed to lack the cohesiveness of the coeducational.

Fairport grammar is a direct grant school of 750 boys (it has a junior school up to the age of eleven, of 250). Founded in 1732, the dignified late eighteenth-century buildings stand in the older part of a famous naval town. There is an air of solidarity and confidence about the place which some would stigmatise as middle-class smugness; yet the bearing and politeness of the boys was impressive, something particularly remarkable in that the interviews had to be conducted out of school teaching hours. Nearly all the boys turned up promptly for the lunchtime and after-school interviews on the basis of a timetable pinned to the form notice-board, and many were prepared to wait for up to an hour after the end of school before they could be seen. Two boys, in particular, who had missed the hour-long I Q test, willingly agreed to take it in their own time. Such attitudes have much to do with home background and not surprisingly the boys come mainly from the 'good' residential areas of the town: the middle-class values of hard work, honesty and 'playing the game' are reinforced and emphasised at school. But though this is the tone which predominates, Fairport grammar does include a cross section of society, 'much more so than some of the neighbourhood comprehensive schools which will come into existence', the senior history master said. 'In our school we have boys of all types; and on the whole they fuse remarkably well. At the end of the year it's remarkably difficult to tell the difference between the average son of the naval officer and the average son of the lorry driver: there are exceptions of course'.

Tradition plays a much larger part in the life of this school than in the other four. For example, it has strong naval and military connections, and these are reflected in the large and well turned out C C F which often represents the school on formal occasions. Though there may be those amongst the staff and boys who feel that this is overdone, most would say that the tradition of the school is an advantage rather than a disadvantage because of the way in which it raises standards and helps to give unity and direction to the community. As the senior history master put it:

'I think that many of our boys do feel a certain amount of loyalty to the school and a certain sense of responsibility, though they wouldn't probably acknowledge this for worlds; but I think they do feel it in their heart of hearts, and in general their conduct outside the school, for example, is somewhat higher than in the case of other local schools. Obviously, from time to time, they let us down; but in general the standard is not too bad and I think that the fact is connected with the tradition of the school.'

A mile and a half or so away, on the edge of this naval town, Neil Grammar School for boys is situated. It presents an interesting contrast to the direct grant school, drawing its 650 boys mainly from a lower

2

middle-class and working-class area. Founded in 1920, it is housed in a rather dreary yet solid and serviceable red brick building which it shares with a girls' grammar school. From the start it was under the control of the local authority. The more obvious traditions seem to exert little influence within the school, though there were encouraging signs of a very active Oxfam group run by some of the younger boys; and in the Easter term of 1966 a lively sixth form group was organising a concert and dance. 'I feel, myself', said the senior history master, 'that we are trying to make tradition play an important part when it doesn't really. But tradition, particularly in a new school like this, is something we build up.'

The boys were charming and cooperative; indeed some of the most worthwhile interviews were held in this school. Perhaps the lack of middle-class inhibitions enabled the pupils to speak up with a directness and candour which was never personal, nor in bad taste, but was often illuminating and refreshing. The boys are less polished (both literally and metaphorically) than those of the direct grant school, but they showed less of that slightly bogus sophistication – a more open and ingenuous approach to life which, for example, made them tackle the research tests with great enthusiasm, though once the papers were completed, they quickly became bored, restless and badly behaved. Understandably, these boys were less complacent about the school curricula they were following: the middle-class conformist pressures were less in evidence; and several of the groups were counting the days until they could leave school. Yet there was a happy-go-lucky cheeriness about the form which was rather endearing; perhaps the more vociferous moaners were not as discontented with their school lot as they made out.

Scarcombe grammar school for girls stands in another large naval town – though its activities stem from the merchant rather than royal navy. The school, which was founded in 1907 and is now under the control of the local authority, has rather imposing neo-Georgian buildings; pleasant gardens and playing fields surround it and across the road the trees and grass of the town common can be seen. History is a very popular subject in the school – the questionnaire replies emphasise this – and observing one or two history lessons confirmed the impression; there was a relaxed friendliness in the classroom which most would find admirable. But in spite of the delightfully free atmosphere, there seems to be a certain pride of place and position about the school which gives it dignity and purposefulness; the school is conscious of its standing in the town and is anxious to maintain its standards of hard work and success in the public examinations.

It was to Scarcombe and the other four schools that I was a frequent visitor between October 1965 and July 1966. My concern of course was with only one aspect of the schools – their history departments; and the paragraphs which follow describe their organisation and equipment.

The heart of any department is formed by the teachers who man it; and table 1 shows the number of history specialists in each school and the length of their experience.

Table 1. History teachers' teaching experience

School	Specialist history teachers	Years of experience	Years in present teaching post	Teaching certificate
Benborough (Mixed)	Head of Department: Mr Black	4	2	yes
	a (man)	5	1	yes
	b (man)	30	3	yes
Daymer (Girls)	Head of Department: Miss Denton	35	24	yes
	a (woman)	18	18	yes
Fairport (Boys)	Head of Department: Mr Freeman	26	19	yes
	a (man)	16	16	yes
	b (man)	10	2	yes
	c (man)	7	1 term	yes
Neil (Boys)	Head of Department: Mr Neville	17	8	yes
	a (man)	12	10	yes
Scarcombe (Girls)	Head of Department: Miss Spender	9	5	no
	a (woman)	3½	3	yes
	b (woman)	3	1	no
	c (woman)	1	1	yes

These are the men and women who cope with the day to day routine of teaching: what are their history teaching commitments throughout the school? Table 2 gives details.

Neither of the girls' schools streams, though pupils at Daymer are put in sets for history in the third year: the other three schools all do. The reaction of the senior history teachers was mixed; none felt strongly in favour of streaming for history. As Mr Freeman put it:

> 'In general I'm for it: though I think the case for setting in history is nothing like so strong as in some other subjects. I don't feel very strongly about this in regard to my own subject.'

Mr Neville had this to say:

> 'In vacuum I disapprove of streaming. I can see no reason academically

for streaming history; and I'd quite like to see a non-academic division of a year into forms, shall we say for history, geography, English literature, even though the language and maths people insist (probably quite rightly) that they do need sets.'

Only Miss Spender came out strongly against streaming.

'I don't think it's necessary to begin with; it tends to make people consider that they are "good" or 'bad', "second grade", "third grade". I think it gives them a lot of wrong values. I just don't think it's necessary.'

Table 2. *Size of schools, number of history periods per week in the first five years and size of history sixth forms in all schools.*

School	Approxi-mate size of school	History periods per week					Pupils in 6th form (1965)		
		1st year	2nd year	3rd year	4th year	5th year	1st year	2nd year	3rd year
Benborough (Mixed)	600	3	A stream 2 B & C streams 3	A & B streams 2½ C & D streams 3	A stream 2½ B & C streams 3	A stream 2½ B & C streams 3	11	14	5
Daymer (Girls)	700	2	2	2½	3	3	16	8	–
Fairport (Boys)	750	3	3	3	3	3	25	30	3
Neil (Boys)	650	3	2	3	3	4	13	10	3
Scarcombe (Girls)	810	3	2	2	4	4	56	31	8

The size of classes in Scarcombe tends to be smaller than the other three – 25 as against 30 and 30 + – and this lends itself to slightly easier disciplinary conditions and more opportunities for group work. As Mr Neville said when asked if he would like to see the size of classes reduced:

'Well, obviously. First, ease of contact: secondly (a selfish point) the smaller the group the easier the discipline is. Thirdly, assuming we still have streaming, the smaller the group, the greater the number of sets in any one year and therefore the greater the homogeneity.'

Mr Black and Miss Denton looked forward to small classes, while Mr Black and Miss Spender emphasised the burden sixth form marking can impose on the history teacher. Mr Black's comment is particularly illuminating:

'I think what happens and where we go wrong is that we teach too much – and this is going to get worse as sixth forms get bigger. You're going to spend more and more time working and less and less

5

time preparing for the lower school. I'm sure that a great many staff who teach a lot of the sixth form work go into the lower school lessons far more often than they would like and think along the corridor of the line the lesson is going to take; and this is forced upon them. One example recently: I met someone with 29 geographers in the upper sixth and 29 geographers in the lower sixth; the forms were not split, he had no second geographer and only four 'bits' of people (this is not in Benborough). This is the sort of situation we're going to get increasingly.'

The three teachers with the longest experience were a little more guarded. Miss Denton replied in answer to the question 'Do you feel over burdened with marking etc. and have insufficient time for reading, preparation?': 'I imagine most staff feel that. One ought to learn to organise things better – but still . . .'; and Mr Neville said that 'There's time for people to do what they *want* to do.' Mr Freeman with twenty-six distinguished years of teaching behind him, spoke of the holidays.

'I wouldn't say we are excessively burdened. Of course, history is a subject which probably involves more time on marking than most subjects. But we have the holidays in which we can do a lot of reading. No, I don't think we ought to make any complaint.'

All pupils at Benborough take history at 'O' level; at Daymer and Fairport the subject becomes optional in the fifth year. When asked if he would like to have all pupils taking history at 'O' level, Mr Freeman replied:

'Not particularly, no. I don't regard "O" level history as a very desirable or essential intellectual discipline: I think I'd go the other way and say that I'd rather no one took it. In fact, supposing the headmaster said to me "We've got to drop history somewhere, where would you like it dropped?" I think I'd probably say, "Well, I'd like to drop it a 'O' level, and have the early schemes of work which we give them, which I think are much more worth while than the ones they do at 'O' level." '

Such an outspoken attack on the 'O' level examination would no doubt be applauded by many history teachers; but Mr Neville voiced an opinion which would weigh heavily with some.

'From the point of view of the benefit to the development of history obviously I think it would be a good thing for all boys to take history at "O" level.'

The bargaining power of a department with headmasters or at staff meetings is enhanced if it holds 'examination' status; and the larger the number of candidates the greater the influence of the subject. Scarcombe allows history to become an option as an examination subject in the fifth year; history is taught as a general subject (one lesson a week) to most fourth and fifth years.

'I don't like their having to choose whether they do history or not for "O" level in the fourth form. Whether I'd like to see them all taking the "O" level exam is a different matter. I'd like to see the possibility of everyone continuing to take history seriously – four or maybe three lessons a week – until the sixth form.'

At Neil the system is complicated. After two years in the school, in alternate years, the A and B streams opt for history and craft or Greek and Spanish; *or* geography and craft or Greek and Spanish. After the third year the C and D streams opt for history or economics. Thus it is possible for a boy to cover only a two year history course.

How important is a specialist room for the teaching of history? All five schools' geography departments have one or more classrooms designed for the teaching of the subject – at Scarcombe there is a geography wing of four classrooms which has recently been built; but history seems to be considered the 'poor relation' by the administrators, tolerated but not encouraged and frequently palmed off with the second best. Mr Freeman said:

'We are not too generously treated in the way of equipment, and I feel a little discontented from time to time in that I have rather to press and agitate even to get an extra cupboard, whereas other departments who have asked for large sums of money have got them rather more easily . . . I think if we could spend £100 (which is far less than has been spent by the language department) we could probably improve things considerably.'

Each of the schools has a room or rooms which are labelled 'history' but they are little more than ordinary classrooms and none of them seems entirely satisfactory. Benborough and Scarcombe, for example, have no blackout (though Miss Spender appended a note that blackout was to be fitted in February 1966); display cupboards are poor or nonexistent in all schools; display boards are poor or inadequate in two schools, only adequate in the remaining three (though again Miss Spender noted that the 'inadequate frieze' was being extended). But suppose their ships came home and lavishly equipped specialist rooms were forthcoming, what effect would it have on the teaching of their subject? Two teachers were fairly certain that it would make little difference.

'. . . I don't think that it is necessary – all we really need is bare walls and a blackboard' (Mr Black).

'I don't think so, and quite honestly I'm not certain that geography is taught any differently because they do have an elaborately equipped geography room. All these things are *aids* and I don't think any specialist teacher who really knows his subject is going to allow the aids to become more important than his subject' (Mr Neville).

Miss Denton and Miss Spender on the other hand, felt that it would be a help.

'It would make life a good deal easier.'

'It would be very nice to have a lavishly equipped room . . . I think what we really lack at the moment is display space and an extra room where people could do preparation and do work of their own not supervised and away from classrooms. This is one thing we lack; but this is an ideal which we'll probably never realise . . . .'

Partly because of these inadequate facilities, equipment such as film projectors, wireless and television is seldom used at the five schools when the total history teaching time is considered. On the other hand, greater use is made of historical material – maps, reproductions of documents (for example, the 'Jackdaw' series), pictures, photographs, sets of books (for example, the 'Then and There' series), and so on. All the schools are well provided with such material, and it seems to be used fairly frequently in class – though only in Scarcombe was there any evidence of documents being studied in the fourth year (the girls, who were learning twentieth-century world affairs, were being encouraged to look for information in Hansard). Frequent use, too, is made of the 'outline' textbook; and most of the schools follow the normal practice of issuing one or sometimes two to each pupil. Neil and Scarcombe have pools of sets of books which the pupil can borrow for short periods, though at Neil an 'outline' is issued for the year.

It would seem, therefore, that the organisation and equipment of the five departments are broadly similar, and the contrasts are of degree rather than kind. The main impression is that the departments are limited by inadequate facilities (in spite of what Mr Black and Mr Neville said) and that if they had properly equipped history rooms the opportunities for more flexible teaching and project and group work would be greater.

Such are the schools and their history departments which provided the material for the investigation. It is this material which the following chapters discuss and use as the basis for a general consideration of secondary school history.

2 The syllabus

We are all familiar with the arguments against teaching history merely through an 'outline' course; familiar too, with the proposals that fourth and fifth year pupils should study twentieth-century history up to the current year and that their syllabus should be world orientated rather than Eurocentric. But however familiar such arguments may be, the problems they present are complex and are still in need of discussion and analysis. It is of course true that there can be no such thing as The Ideal Syllabus – the complete answer for all secondary schools; and to a certain extent the history course must be tailormade for the particular situation. However, the practice of other history teachers can be of value in clarifying our thinking; and in this chapter the problems of constructing syllabuses dealing with world and twentieth-century history, and the general criteria for the selection of material, are examined from the points of view of the teachers who helped in this research. The pupils give their comments in the second section. In the third section conclusions are drawn and tentative recommendations made.

THE TEACHERS SPEAK

The five schools submitted syllabuses of varying lengths, and those for the first three years are summarised in table 3. The GCE syllabuses and the fourth and fifth years are dealt with separately.

One aspect of our educational system that is often considered a matter for congratulation is the amount of freedom of choice of material the classroom teacher is given. This is particularly so in the first three years of

Table 3. History syllabuses for first three years – all schools

School	Year 1	Year 2	Year 3
BENBOROUGH	3 periods per week	A stream 2 periods per week B & C streams 3 periods per week	A & B streams 2½ periods per week C & D streams 3 periods per week
	Early times – 1485 Early civilisation Roman Britain Norman Britain Feudalism	1485 – *c.* 1660 Renaissance and Reformation Voyages of discovery General outline of English history	*c.* 1660 – *c.* 1815 English history: political, economic and social developments

9

Table 3—continued

	2 periods per week	2 periods per week	2½ periods per week
DAYMER	Early and medieval man and his environment 1. Prehistory and stories of ancient world 2. Brief survey of Greek–Roman times: end of Roman Empire 3. Middle Ages to c. 1450	Early modern period emphasising adventure and discoveries and man's growing spirit of enquiry and knowledge Renaissance: Tudor Monarchs Early Stuarts	1. Main topics of late 17th and 18th century English history 2. Economic and social changes 18th and early 19th centuries 3. Civics – Local government; Parliament and central government
	3 periods per week	**3 periods per week**	**3 periods per week**
FAIRPORT	Recap – Romans, Saxons, Conquest – English history through topics 1066 – 1485. Emphasis on local history[1]	Tudors and Stuarts through topics Emphasis on local history	Removes B, C, D 1689 – 1815 through topics Emphasis on local history 5a rapid stream 1689 – 1851. A rapid version of remove syllabus with less attention to certain topics
	3 periods per week	**2 periods per week**	**3 periods per week**
NEIL	Development of civilisations: India, China. Rise and fall of Rome. Christianity and Islam. Civilisation of High Middle Ages. Eastern civilisation	Renaissance, Reformation Overseas expansion of Europe Beginnings of nation states Europe, the arbiter of the world. The Dynasts. Struggle for freedom – England, U.S.A., France, India. Growth of industry, democracy. From World War to World Government	U.S.S.R. U.S.A.

[1] Mr Freeman said in the interview that 'the lower school has just [Jan. 1966] changed its syllabus to cover the Ancient World, Romans, Anglo-Saxons, Danes and Normans. We take over with the Angevins.'

Table 3—continued

	3 periods per week	2 periods per week	2 periods per week
SCARCOMBE	Ancient civilisations: Sumer, Egypt, Greece, Rome, Indus Valley, China. Medieval Europe: topics: fall of Rome, Pre-conquest Britain, Organisation of society	Renaissance, Reformation, Elizabethan state. Life of Cromwell. Pepys's London, St Simon's Versailles. Industrial Revolution. Agriculture, 18th and 19th centuries	French Revolution; American Revolution, and Civil War. 19th century Europe – Vienna settlement – nationalist revolts – Creation of Germany to 1914. European colonising. 19th century England – topics to illustrate development of modern constitutions

the secondary school, before the external examination has cast its shadow. The history syllabuses of the group therefore are intended to serve as guides rather than directives; and the heads of departments made it clear that the topics within the broad frameworks are the responsibility of the individual class teachers. Such responsibility may, perhaps, for some of the younger teachers be too great to bear, particularly in the first, hectic year of teaching; it may also mean that there is less cohesion within the department which can lead to a lack of clarity as to methods and goals. The nature of the subject is largely to blame for this. It is nebulous and illdefined, and superficially, at any rate, a partial understanding of one period or topic can be achieved without knowing much about previous or subsequent periods. Nevertheless, the syllabus frameworks try to present a logical and cohesive picture; and the tacit hope of the senior history teachers is that this sense of 'l'histoire' rather than 'les histoires' is conveyed to the separate classes.

The syllabuses divide into two groups: first, Benborough, Daymer and Fairport which follow what can loosely be called the traditional syllabus – English chronological history from early times to the twentieth-century; second, Neil and Scarcombe grammar schools, which have adopted a more cosmopolitan outlook and have tried to put Britain into a world setting[1]. In all schools local history is dealt with to a certain extent in the

---

[1] The pupils from Neil grammar school who took part in the research had in fact been following a more conventional syllabus than the one outlined in table 3. They were the last course not to have started the new syllabus. Briefly, the course these boys had covered is as follows: year 1 – World and English history to 1066; year 2 – England and Europe to 1485; year 3 – England and Europe to 1789; year 4 – first half, French Revolution, second half, 'O' level syllabus.

first three or four years, though it seems that more is made of it at Fairport and Scarcombe (these two schools are particularly lucky in being situated in towns rich with local historical material). Local history, however, is something which is very much a matter of personal taste. The debate on world history is a more urgent one and was something which concerned all five teachers.

Mr Black mentioned the difficulty of broadening the syllabus:

'The dilemma, of course, is time, isn't it? It's a question of whether you do a little well, or a lot superficially. I think there is a very great case for widening the traditional grammar school syllabus which concentrates too much on English history. I think the difficulties are in forms one and two, say, or even in the third form; English history has some particular meaning for them. You haven't got to justify it particularly, whereas if you're looking at Polish history, perhaps you have . . . I think we must get away from English history in time.'

Miss Denton expressed some scepticism:

'I think it's very difficult to make a general survey unless you've got some detail to make it understandable . . .'

while Mr Freeman said he was intending to alter his syllabus to cover a wider field:

'I think we should include more world history – but the difficulty again is selection. One has got to present it in such a way that the boy feels committed to it. Inevitably in world history one will be dealing with wider generalisations and these are often more difficult for the less able boy to grasp. But I don't believe that national or local history should be squeezed out by world history; perhaps the balance should be thirty-three and a third of each. I do think that we must inculcate a sense of patriotism – at any rate a sense of commitment to society. Perhaps it's lack of this that is the trouble with many young people today.'

When Mr Neville was asked what made him change to a world orientated syllabus he replied:

'Part of it is that British history is not adequate for 1965 and that we must think in bigger terms and realise that England and Western Europe are *not* the fulcrum of the world. Secondly, the impacts that are now being made on us by other cultures; and thirdly, and practically, I thought I'd like a change.'

Miss Spender had this to say about her syllabus.

'I think this business of world understanding is very important, although this is a cliché. But the insularity of just teaching British history which has gone on for so long I think is appalling for this reason: it does mean that there are even more barriers in peoples' minds to understanding other ways of thinking, other attitudes to life, other religions than their own. And they'll be shocked if they go outside this country. I'm not thinking of comparing but appreciating and valuing for its own sake.'

Such a statement carried conviction with its sincerity; but the problem of selection remains. For example, the second year pupils at Scarcombe, who are given only two periods of history a week, have a formidable area of history to cover and individual teachers will have to be ruthless in what

Table 4. G C E *ordinary level history syllabuses – all schools*

School	Board	Syllabus	Time spent
BENBOROUGH	London	2 forms – British history 1763 – 1832: 1832 – 1914 1 form – British history 1832 – 1914 European history 1830 – 1914	6 terms (A stream 2½ periods per week B and C streams 3)
DAYMER	Oxford	Better divisions: British and foreign 1870 – 1939 Weaker divisions: British social and economic history 1760 – 1939.	c. 4½ terms 6 terms (3 periods per week)
FAIRPORT	Cambridge	British and foreign history 1815 – 1939	Rapid stream c. 4½ terms Other streams 6 terms (3 periods per week)
NEIL	Oxford	British history 1815 – 1939	4½ terms (3 periods per week)
SCAR-COMBE	London	World affairs 1919 to present day	6 terms (4 periods per week)

they leave out. Neil grammar school's syllabus for the second year is even longer and it seems unlikely that the course can be covered in the time available.

A more stereotyped picture emerges when the G C E syllabuses are inspected: these are summarised in table 4. The pupils seem to be spending the best part of the fourth and fifth years on 'O' level work. They may, as for example in Daymer, cover an outline of the G C E course in the fourth year, 'in order to provide some knowledge of the nineteenth and twentieth-centuries for those girls who will not continue history after the fourth year' and to give a basis of knowledge for further work in the fifth form for those who will be taking history at 'O' level. One fourth year form at Fairport is doing an experimental course entitled 'The birth of the modern world' which includes many of the topics to be covered for 'O' level but aims at giving a wider picture. The boys of Neil grammar school spend one and a half terms in the fourth year on economic history before moving on to the 'O' level syllabus. Benborough and Scarcombe move straight into the G C E course.

The choice of 'O' level syllabus is varied and all the G C E boards whose examinations the five schools take, offer papers which cover, for example, the most recent periods. The opportunity to bring the school history syllabus up to date is there: what are the opinions of the senior history teachers? Miss Spender was convinced that world history 1919 to the present day is not only vitally important but more relevant and therefore more acceptable to the girls. Miss Denton was more sceptical about modern history's popularity.

'When I said to my present fifth form that we were going to con-centrate on the most recent period (you'll notice that I've recently changed the syllabus from 1815 – 1939 to 1870 – 1939 but with a wider survey within that period) they weren't very pleased, rather to my dismay. I've found recently that girls are not so keen about doing recent history as they used to be – recent history is around them too much of the time or something.'

Mr Neville had another point of view.

'Anything which happened more than twenty years ago – certainly more than fifty years ago – is probably just as far away to the boys as anything which happened 5,000 years ago. But on the other hand, the point about reading modern history is that in most other eras things have moved fairly leisurely. Think of the colossal changes in the last 150 years. There have been other years of fairly rapid change – I suppose the results of the work of Alexander of Macedon; but in those days things didn't alter very much for the ordinary person. Nowadays, of course, they're changing rapidly for everyone so that it might be argued that we ought to give some idea of the speed of change today so that people at school might be a little more able to understand the differences between their thought and their parents' thought. Now this is the only reason that I can think of for teaching modern history rather than any other. Take one example here. If a boy of fifteen has a father of forty his approach to problems like job mobility is going to be very different from that of his father; and I think it wouldn't be a bad idea if he knew why.'

Such an argument seems logical. The events of the 1950s and 1960s are not necessarily more relevant to a pupil because they happened within his own lifetime; often they will have as little interest as last week's paper.

Mr Neville argues that if recent history is to be taught, it must be taught for the historical understandings it can give and not merely because it deals with the twentieth century.

The teaching of twentieth-century history poses particular problems. In the first place there is the sheer volume of material the teacher has to cope with, and the need for rigorous selection is imperative. Secondly, there is the effect of the syllabus on the first three years. 'It's a question of time,' said Mr Black. 'If you're trying to get up to 1965 everything in the lower school becomes stretched; again you're even more dependent on selection. It puts a great onus on the teacher.'

In other words, the syllabus in the first few years must be speeded up in order to reach the twentieth century by the beginning of the fifth year. Now such a statement implies that the chronological aspect of history is of paramount importance and that one of the duties of the history teacher is to convey the sense of time and development – that is, the linear quality of history. Certainly all five syllabuses are based on a developing time scale; and it seemed important to find out how far the teachers consider and stress this aspect of the subject. Miss Spender made it clear that she places little importance on chronological history. The syllabus is eclectic rather than chronologically cohesive and this enables the department to be teaching twentieth-century history by the fourth year. Mr Black, in spite of his chronologically orientated syllabus, lays little stress on the time element.

'I think if I'm absolutely honest I don't think it is important except in a very general pattern of progress from somewhere to now. The making of a time chart doesn't particularly appeal to me and of itself is not particularly valuable unless you want to hammer some point home into its historical perspective. As long as there emerges a general idea of change and progress (whatever that means) this I find satisfactory. I'm sure a lot of people disagree with me violently';

and Miss Denton said:

'Well, I suppose it's important but in practice whatever one does children are too young to be expected to have a great deal of time sense. I feel it beginning to emerge after the fifth year. . .'

'But with eleven-year-olds – a 1000 years or 10 years; it's all in the past?', I asked. 'Yes – it doesn't make much difference. I think at the time one is pushing it home it means something but it ceases to fairly soon after.'

Mr Neville felt that the essential thing was to get across some idea that things develop and there has got to be something which goes before. Now so long as these views are held the need for a rigidly chronological 'early times to the present day' syllabus becomes very much less, and there seems no logical reason for dashing through the centuries in order to give a complete picture and many arguments against it, the most obvious being that history taught at a high level of generality is difficult to grasp and consequently tedious for the pupils. On the other hand, Mr Freeman was clear that the teaching of a time sense is important: 'I think it is important and I think it should be done. Perhaps one shouldn't bother excessively about it in the first year, or even maybe in the second; but I think by about the third year one should actually do this.'

Whether or not the chronology of history is stressed, all the teachers have to face the problems of choice of material. Selection, of course, takes place at different levels. There is the broad selection which has to be made when a syllabus is drawn up; there is the more immediate selection within the syllabus framework for the term's work; and (perhaps most important of all) there is the selection of material for a particular lesson. It was difficult for the teachers to distinguish between these three levels and their comments were of a general nature which embraced all aspects. All used the word 'interest' – the teacher's interest and the pupils'.

'I think it divides into the magic pre "O" level period and the equally magic after "O" level period,' said Mr Black. 'In years one, two, and three, within the "date range" (it sounds horrible) I select what will interest them and from which they can get as full an idea as possible of the pattern of life at that time and the importance of that particular event.

'I try to make it a mixture of what I think is important they should know as future citizens of this country and what they'll be interested in as girls of the age they are' (Miss Denton).

This is what Mr Neville had to say about the criterion of interest:

'In the early forms I think the main criterion should be interest. Obviously one's got to modify this in some measure, for presumably if you thought only of interest you'd make up a syllabus consisting entirely of executions, murders, war and so on. So clearly this theme of interest has got to be modified by some form of historical balance. But the fact remains to my mind that it matters very little in the early school what one teaches provided that one does in fact stir their interest, and provided that one encourages them to relate what they learn in school to what they see outside; that one does encourage them to develop a taste for themselves. I'm sure this is true, for I have from time to time given tests to boys in the first year sixth on the history they've done in the last five years – fifty questions; and believe me, the results are extremely depressing. It's quite incredible how quickly they forget things they had learned for a particular examination. Boys will forget, say, the statutes of Gladstone's first ministry which they'd know absolutely – they'd learned really hard; twelve months later the facts will have completely gone. Well, my conclusion from all this is that it doesn't really matter very much what the content is provided you have stimulated interest, and moreover, if you've managed to relate it to some living thing or experience – to a visit or something they've read or done – it's much more likely that they will retain things. This has come out of my tests. The things that they have retained have always invariably been linked to some actual activity rather than subjects which have just been learned *in vacuo* as it were.' Miss Spender also stressed interest: 'As little political history as possible in the junior school; what interests the members of staff who are teaching most. This syllabus is a bit loose; and it's developed out of the interests of the four of us.'

Mr Neville mentioned interest among other factors:

'This is not in any particular order: comprehensibility to the boy; importance in the historical process; juvenile interest; and I think probably too (this is a very awkward way of saying it) those periods or topics which have a moral or teaching significance – moral is the wrong word here – those topics, in fact, from which it's possible to *learn* something.'

This emphasis on interest is hardly surprising; like patriotism, however, it is not enough, as Mr Freeman emphasised. If it becomes the dominating criterion there is a danger that the subject turns into a game and its discipline goes by the board. But it is not particularly helpful to rely on phrases such as 'importance of the event', 'historical balance' or 'importance in the historical process', for it is difficult, if not impossible, to gain a concensus of opinion as to what constitute the important facts of history. There are of course certain topics which most British teachers feel they have a duty to teach. As Mr Black said:

'Certain topics select themselves against your better judgment. For example . . . in the second year I think somewhere, somehow, the reformation has to come in, if only superficially, because otherwise this will never be done and they'll never hear of Old Luther and that sort of thing . . .'

'And somehow we feel we've failed if they go up to the senior school without knowing who Martin Luther was,' I added.

'This is perhaps a guilt complex we shouldn't have', he replied.

Thus, for example, all five teachers teach the Renaissance in the second year, presumably because they feel that it is a seminal period, a period in which much of the old is put in the melting pot and modern Europe begins to be hammered out. But what a wide field for manoeuvre this still leaves! There are endless ways in which the 'quattrocento' can be treated and many interpretations. Few today share the optimism of Acton and the late nineteenth- and early twentieth-century historians that Ultimate History can be written; and the five teachers would feel happier perhaps with E. H. Carr's theory of the interaction between the historian and the facts – that it is the duty of the historian to select, structure and breathe life into the dry bones; to present not The Answer, but an answer, a facet of the truth. Indeed, if they accept the premise that complete objectivity can never be achieved, then the choice that lies before them is either to accept the interpretation of some official organisation (as, for example, historians had to in the Third Reich) or to rely on their own interpretation of the facts.

The implications of this for school history are important. For it seems that outside a general framework it is unlikely that agreement will be reached on the more detailed content of the syllabus. Such disagreement and contrasts were shown by the teachers in their answers to Question 27 of the questionnaire (see App. I, p. 127) which deals in tabular form with the particular orientation of their syllabuses. They were asked to assess on a five point scale the emphasis they placed in the different years on the various branches of history.

All five teachers found difficulty in filling in the table with honesty and accuracy. Miss Spender wrote (in a letter acknowledging receipt of the questionnaire);

> 'I've looked – with horror! – at your latest magnum opus. So far I've pencilled in the straightforward stuff at the beginning but at No. 27 I give up . . . First, as you will probably agree, one is not conscious while teaching of the subdivisions and certainly not of their relative importance. Second, though one may be convinced that the development of religious ideas may be of great importance in sixteenth-century England one would not necessarily introduce this to second formers. Thirdly, by the very selectiveness of the syllabus many of the sections on the list may be omitted from any one or all four years. In other words I cannot fit your question on to what we teach. So we must talk about that one! However, I will do my best to complete the document . . . If you can elucidate I'd be glad.'

This frank attitude was typical of the five teachers. They saw the difficulties, they struggled to give some sort of response to the table. Miss Spender's criticism is justified; but the picture which emerged from the answers was useful and in the interviews it was possible to explore the teachers' answers more fully.

The question produced a diversity of response. A few examples will serve to illustrate this point. Miss Spender considers religious ideas and beliefs 'important' in the fourth and fifth years; Miss Denton considers them 'unimportant'; Mr Black and Mr Neville left the entry boxes blank. Mr Freeman wrote: 'I find it impossible to deal with this subject (religion) by ticks. My answer would depend on the nature of the topic.'

Mr Freeman thinks the growth of the British constitution 'should not be done' in the fifth years; Mr Black, Miss Denton and Mr Neville have rated it 'important'; Miss Spender has left the entry box blank. Now such contrasts are partly and obviously explained by the nature of the syllabus. By the fifth year Miss Spender is dealing with World Affairs since 1919 and presumably the British constitution's development plays a minimal part. Similarly, Miss Denton is dealing with the 'O' level syllabus in the fifth year – nineteenth- and twentieth-century Britain – and therefore she feels she has little time for religious digression because this sort of information is seldom required in the examination, whereas questions on the parliamentary reform bills are standard fare and turn up with regularity. But in spite of these obvious explanations, some of the emphases or omissions throw light on the teachers' philosophy. For example, all tend to stress social history in the first three years. 'Up to the fifth form that is what appeals more and is most easily graspable', said Miss Denton. '. . . Social history is what people in the lower school can most easily comprehend. It is more or less within their own experience' (Mr Neville). Mr Freeman modified his questionnaire answer by saying:

'In our first year I think we stress social history rather more strongly; but in the other years (I don't know how far we succeed) we endeavour to produce a reasonable balance. Let me take an example: I was talking to Gordon (a student teacher) just before you came, about work he's going to do with a third year form. Let me briefly go through what he will be doing with them. I started them off at the beginning of term by doing Jacobitism with them – the '15' and '45'. I expect you'd call that a political topic, wouldn't you? He will then as his first subject next week do Parson Woodforde; and the object there will be to establish the way of life in an eighteenth-century Norfolk village and in particular the life of a country parson in such a village. Well, obviously, this would be a social topic. Now the third topic for the term will almost certainly be the mid-century wars and particularly the struggle for empire with special stress on the personalities – Clive and India, Wolfe and Quebec . . . Hawke and Boscawen, and Pitt. This then is of a political, military and to some extent personal nature. After that I shall try to persuade him to do a social topic. One topic we often do is the Whig nobleman taking as our example the Duke of Bedford and especially the building of Woburn. . . . I suppose you'd call that a social and economic topic. Then we'll probably cover the American revolution after that which would be a political topic. We've already done John Wesley which was a religious topic. So my aim here, in this particular year, is to produce a reasonable balance.'

This senior history teacher's comment has been quoted in full because it seems to highlight a fairly general attitude: in the first three years topics are chosen for their colour or interest rather than their ability to illustrate a particular aspect of history; and the fact that these can very often be called 'social' is more a reflection of the broad interpretation of the word than an indication that 'social history' as such has consciously been taught. This, of course, is not always so; and, for example, in the third, fourth and fifth years Mr Neville considers economic history 'very important'. His interest obviously lies in this direction (see, for example, his syllabus); presumably he makes a point during these years of choosing topics which illustrate the material and financial development of mankind. Miss Spender, a gifted pianist, makes a particular point of cultural and artistic topics in the first two years. Mr Freeman considers local historical topics 'important' throughout the five years. Mr Neville, who taught R E at one time, stated that he thought the story of religion in Britain, Europe and the religions of the world were 'important' in the second year. By and large, therefore, the picture of these salad days is one of contrasts in which teachers follow their own interests and the interests and assumed needs of their pupils without feeling committed to any aspect, or indeed, to any rigid plan. When, in the fourth year, the G C E syllabus is begun, room for manoeuvre becomes less. Political and economic topics feature more frequently, local history less prominently. Most of the teachers certainly find the restrictions the examination syllabus imposes irksome; and there was a tendency for them to look back nostalgically to the first three years when they had free rein to explore what paths they liked.

These then are the syllabuses the senior history teachers have adopted. The paragraphs which follow look at the problems of course construction and selection of material from a different angle – the pupils'.

THE PUPILS SPEAK

It is not the intention of this section to take the pupils' *obiter dicta* too seriously, for by the nature of things their comments on the syllabus stem from an imperfect understanding of the issues at stake. However, as the senior history teachers made clear, we all take the interests of the pupils into account when constructing syllabuses; and because apathy or anti-pathy to the subject is most prevelant in the fourth and fifth years, it is right to pay some attention to their views.

The majority of pupils considered that world history rather than national history should be taught. They gave a variety of reasons for their affirmative answers. A number took the line of 'anything to get away from the British syllabus'; many adopted a more positive approach. The following comments came from the questionnaires.

' . . . national history cannot be understood if taught on its own. It is always connected with other countries in some way and therefore world history would give a fuller picture of life' (Girl, Benborough G S).

'I think it is important because when you travel and go abroad it is useful to know the history of the country you're visiting' (Daymer G S).

'If national history is taught, then the feeling of self importance can creep in especially in this country. I think both national and world history ought to be taught' (Fairport G S).

'I think so because one should know and understand what has happened in other countries so that one can compare it with our own country's history' (Neil G S).

'History is associated with the world as a whole. It does not stop at frontiers. There are constantly wars, marriages, arguments between nations' (Scarcombe G S).

'When there has been a war for example one side always teaches in history that it was the other's fault. I believe that if world history were taught people would understand this kind of thing more' (S G S).

'If we only learned national history we would lose the sense of proportion of our country with the rest of the world and we *might* feel that our country is best and always right' (s g s).

Three comments from Scarcombe grammar school's questionnaires have been given because the weight of opinion here was so heavily in favour of the broad syllabus. It is easy to dismiss some of these pupils' remarks as trite clichés, opinions the girls have perhaps overheard and use now as appropriate for the questionnaire. But many rang true; and it did seem that the world affairs syllabus Scarcombe has adopted is making its impact.

Those who spoke against world history had two main lines of argument: either that it would be too difficult, or that national history is more important. Often the first is an irrational attitude based on ignorance as the following conversation shows. I was asking a boy a question about China in the nineteenth century; did he think she had good medical facilities? He replied: 'Well, I mean, does anyone know? I don't think anyone knows. It's like Russia.

MB: Would you like to learn more about Chinese history?

BOY: I should think it would be *very* difficult. Is it very difficult sir?'

Others mentioned the difficulty of foreign names. When a boy from Benborough was asked whether he would like to learn more world history he avoided the question by saying: 'I think we'll have to deal with European history which is coming in next year.'

MB: Are you looking forward to that?

BOY (*dourly*): History's history; but it means there's more awkward names to learn . . .'

A boy from Fairport held the same opinion: 'The names are far harder to learn. . . . The spelling's difficult.'

Quantity was thought to be a difficulty and several of the pupils feared that the subject, already burdened with facts and dates, would become unmanageable.

'There's enough to learn about Britain on its own without having to learn about other places at the same time', wrote a girl from Benborough.

'World history is too great a syllabus to allow it to be done in any depth' (F G S).

'I think that to cover world history would mean too much work and consequently getting mixed up' (N G S).

'It would take too long to get even a basic picture of world history', wrote a girl from Scarcombe, one of the few in that school who was not so enthusiastic about learning world history.

These pupils have obviously taken 'world history' at its face value and feel dismayed by the amount of learning complete coverage would demand.

Those who took the view that national history is more important seemed to feel that this was self evident.

'It makes history more interesting if it is about your country' (F G S).

'National history is more important and more interesting because it concerns our own country and ancestors' (Girl, B G S).

While a boy from Neil G S wrote in a large laborious hand: 'World history is for history fans whereas national history should interest everyone.'

Such objections, though not without some justice, can be overcome by skilful selection and presentation. The next decade will see the broadening of many school history syllabuses as more teachers realise the necessity of awakening in the child what Teilhard de Chardin calls the senses of spatial immensity, of depth, of number, of proportion, of quality, of movement and of the organic; senses which have allowed and will allow 'man to discover man and take his measure'.[1] National history is too limited to fulfil this function; it produces that shortened view which allowed one boy to write: 'I have never really thought about other parts of the world besides Europe.'

World history and recent history are often closely connected: those teachers (such as Miss Spender) who have broadened their syllabuses tend to concentrate on the twentieth century because of the growing inter-dependence of countries during this period. The questionnaire tried to make a distinction and in question 16 asked: 'Do you think that the history of our own times (e.g. 1918 – 66) is more important than distant history?' Over sixty per cent of the pupils answered in the affirmative. Many seemed to think that an understanding of recent events would help them to take their place in today's world. One boy wrote:

'One day we will be citizens with a vote, maybe even government officials. It is therefore essential to go out into the world with a sound knowledge of contemporary events.'

'Helps us to understand our environment', wrote a girl from Scarcombe.

'It is more interesting because it does not seem so unreal and is often connected with your surroundings' (Girl, B G S).

Again, such remarks from the questionnaires are cliché-ridden; and there was more the ring of truth from the several who seemed to think, rather touchingly, that knowledge of contemporary history would provide a talking point with older people.

'When older people begin to talk about the war we are in ignorance since we know nothing about it. It would be much better if we learned about recent things' (Girl, B G S).

'Obviously one should have a knowledge of the history of one's home country to take part in a sensible conversation' (Boy, B G S).

'Because it is better to know the situation of the country nowadays as previous difficulties have been overcome and are finished with. Also in this period of about fifty to sixty years is our, or our parents' and

[1] P. Teilhard de Chardin; *The Phenomenon of Man.* Fontana edn, 1965 p. 37.

22

grandparents', era and it is nice to know something about what they often talk' (D G S).

'This is the period in which our parents and grandparents were living and this is their kind of world. Also, it shows us what led up to the present situation' (F G S).

This lack of communication was mentioned in the interviews. I was discussing with two boys what they would like to do for 'O' level if they had a choice. One was interested in medieval history (partly for reasons of laziness, for he informed me that 'there's less to learn. The further you go back the less things have been recorded'); but the other wanted to study the last twenty years or so. 'I'd sooner do the recent period. You hear more about it – it's everyday talk: whereas no one goes around talking about the battle of Waterloo or what have you every day'. Others talked about the period being more 'real' to them (that is, more credible) because of the evidence of television or in the newspapers; some emphasised the important inventions of the twentieth century; one boy wrote tersely: 'Past is past and best forgotten.'

What had those to say who answered 'No' or 'Don't know' to question 16? One or two pupils showed a clear understanding of the semantic difficulties of the question.

'All history through the ages is as important as modern day history. There can be no comparison' (F G S).

'I think all history is important – to explain why people have become the way they are today' (S G S).

'I don't know that it is important, but I think that it should be taught so that we can compare the different times and see how the world has grown and altered in knowledge, population, etc. Many young people of our own age have surprisingly little knowledge of the 1st and 2nd World Wars, the events etc., I feel, and of comparative events in other countries' (D G S).

Others seemed to think that they had enough modern history at home without being taught it at school as well, and there were a number of comments similar to this: 'You hear and see a lot about 1918 – 1966 from your family and on television but hardly ever do you hear about distant history' (D G S).

What conclusions can one draw from all this? The case for recent history is not overwhelming, though the majority of this group said they felt it is important; and many declared that they would like to be studying it for 'O' level. Some might consider such a preference to be an indication of restlessness and dissatisfaction with the present syllabuses rather than of any real conviction that recent history is more worthwhile. But the enthusiasm of the Scarcombe girls and the attitude of most of the research group pupils would indicate that school history might become more acceptable to fourth and fifth year children if their syllabuses were designed to include recent history.

The pupils' opinions on world and recent history were for the most part speculative; they wrote and spoke with more assurance about their attitudes to topics within their present syllabus framework.

All were fairly insistent that if a topic had a story to tell it was acceptable; if it was a question of dates, acts and reforms that could not be fitted into a pattern then the topic was rejected as 'boring'. As one boy wrote with feeling about the topics he had enjoyed that year: 'Crimean war and Indian mutiny. They are not boring like a lot of history work. A different thing happens all the time whereas with Peel or Pitt all they do is make laws, pass acts and in general bore me.' Laws and acts: dour Gladstones and joyless Peels slaving away at their leglislation in order to bore generations of school children: it's a rather forbidding picture. The theme however repeats itself consistently throughout the five schools in the explanations of topics disliked in the fourth year course.

'French revolution: Mines and factories and their conditions. There were so many dates of different acts and battles which were very muddling' (D G S).

'. . . political matters. The political matters seem to drag on and on and contradict themselves and it appears that they chop and change from one part of the law to another etc.' (F G S).

'Parliamentary reform bills, factory acts. There were so many of them, all in different years each with different reforms. Each has a different date and different causes and different results' (N G S).

'Welfare state, insurance benefits etc. Learning about sickness benefit, pensions, unemployment pay etc. was boring; this was just a set of dates and acts passed in parliament' (S G S).

Yet it is not necessarily the content of the topic which causes the boredom but the way it has been presented. If a topic can be made relevant then the pupils will accept it. 'Relevance', however, is often defined in terms of 'connection with the present' – hence, presumably, the stress on contemporary history: this is possibly too limited an interpretation. For children a topic becomes relevant if in some way it makes an impact. It may be the story which excites the imagination; it may be the actors who provoke admiration, sympathy, hatred; or it may be that it is linked with present institutions or happenings. In each case the topic has been apprehended and appropriated and, whatever its chronological date, has been made, to borrow Croce's idea, 'contemporary history'. Thus in Fairport certain political topics were enjoyed because of the way they illuminated.

'Responsible and representative government. Because I am interested in the way this country is run and the type of government, the powers of the Queen and cabinet etc.'

'Queen's power in England compared with parliament: responsible and representative government. I am interested in the decline of the crown.'

'Politics. It is rather interesting to find out how one's country is run as I enjoy politics.'

Several boys from Neil G S enjoyed the French revolution, and one boy's remark is revealing. 'This was because they were more exciting and easier to understand and it was not factual history. I also think the way we studied it made me like it.' In other words, presentation is all important.

Familiarity with a topic, too, was often cited as a reason for enjoyment. This could take the form of 'because I have heard a lot about the war etc. from old friends and parents and I have seen films e.g. *The Black Fox*' (girl from S G S on Hitler and Germany); or 'because my mother used to live in South Africa, and I was interested in it' (boy from F G S on Cecil Rhodes); or 'mainly because I have studied it at primary school. This was only a little study but was enough to arouse interest when the topic was covered again' (boy from B G S on the Crimean war).

The impression given by these last three comments is that pupils enjoy meeting topics they have already come across in different circumstances – every history teacher knows how eager boys and girls can be to volunteer information about the period they are studying. There is partly the feeling of superiority which the possession of such knowledge gives the child; partly, too, the joy of anticipating the end of the story. In the interviews a pupil showed a similar attitude. The girl had indicated that she enjoyed learning about the Tudors and Stuarts (incidentally, a popular topic with many of the pupils) and gave as her reason: 'Well, Tudors and Stuarts we did for ages: we did that in the junior school – and so I enjoy it.'

The pupils were asked about the topics they had learned during their first three years at grammar school; once again it would seem that most topics can be made interesting if presented in the right manner. For example, 'early man' and 'Egyptian', 'Greek' and 'Roman civilisations' were particularly popular with the girls of Daymer; and the explanation perhaps lies in the following statement:

'I enjoyed the first three years of history because the mistress teaching me made me work. She also made all the topics as interesting as possible. She was not harsh but she did not allow the lesson to become boring. Also I enjoyed Greek, Babylonian, Roman and Egyptian civilisation.'

A number of pupils however wrote that 'early civilisations' or 'early man' were parts of history that they enjoyed most.

'My choice in No. 9 really should include all the early civilisations as I find the study of them both interesting and the facts about them fairly easy to learn, also there are less dates in this period and what dates there are usually approximations: convenient round figures' (Boy, B G S).

'I found the topic very interesting as some things could not be explained and also because I found learning about ancient customs and religions enjoyable' (Girl, B G S).

'Because on that topic we did more drawings and maps, now we just carry on writing' (N G S).

'Man has evolved from animals and early man led a life very similar to that of the animals he hunted and this made his life interesting to study, learning how man's intelligence gradually pulled him up and he became civilised' (N G S).

The interviews gave the opportunity to explore this interest more fully. At Daymer one girl made it clear that it was the teacher who had made the lessons interesting, a comment which gives added weight to the statement already quoted. Another pupil from the same school declared that she would like to study very ancient or very modern history for 'O' level. 'All the rest in the middle is more or less the same; it's a bit boring. The ancient is so very much more different; and you've got to know something about the modern, haven't you?'

A girl from Scarcombe, too, seemed to have had her imagination fired by the first year history; and would like to be studying the early civilisations for G C E. 'In the first year we did Egypt and things like that and I enjoyed it.'

MB: Why? It seems an awfully long time ago, and doesn't seem to have much relevance.

GIRL: Well, it's interesting, especially the way they pickled people'.

A boy from Fairport emphasised the importance of method rather than content when he spoke about what he would prefer to study for G C E – the palaeolithic period. 'You can read about Tudors and Stuarts in books – it's all been discovered; but there's a lot more scope for oneself to discover stuff and analyse the life from archaeology and that sort of thing.'

MB: You don't think you'd find it too confusing if you didn't have the guide lines of a book?

BOY: No, I think it would be all right . . . it would be more difficult I suppose, but it would be very interesting. You'd have more to show for it by the time you'd finished.

Here it seems that the chance for independent activity and for getting to grips with the stuff of history is what attracts.

Of course, this interest in the early civilisations may be nostalgia, emphasising discontent with the G C E year. I suggested this might be the case to two boys from Benborough who said they 'wouldn't mind doing something on ancient civilisations for G C E.' One replied: 'I don't know necessarily if that's the reason; but I like to know how the different races started', a feeling which seemed to be shared by a number of pupils.

The voyages of discovery were popular with many of the pupils; and the Renaissance attracted quite a number, particularly at Scarcombe. This perhaps reflects the importance Miss Spender places on the cultural and artistic aspects of history in the first two years. Elizabethan England too was popular though more so, perhaps, with the girls than the boys; but the fact that at Benborough (a mixed school) rather more boys than girls stated they enjoyed this topic indicates that the sex differences in this context is not a real one, and that presentation is the deciding factor.

It seemed to be worth considering how far such a conclusion is valid for other topics. In Benborough there appeared to be no difference between the fourth year topic choices of the boys and girls. The Crimean war and the Indian mutiny were popular; political topics ('Tory and Whig reforms', 'Chartism') unpopular. In the interviews I asked a number of these pupils whether there are topics which boys enjoy more than girls. Nearly all seemed surprised by the question; they had not considered the matter before. One boy said: 'I think there is to a certain extent. The girls like the parliament side: we like the battle side of it', but there was little spoken evidence from the school to support this opinion.

An interesting commentary came when talking with a group of four pupils, two boys and two girls. I had asked them whether they found that boys and girls had particular topic preferences. The conversation went like this:

GIRL: No, when we were younger in the first form the boys wanted to do the battles more than the girls. But not any more now.

MB: You don't find this as a point of conflict or difficulty?

ALL: No.

MB: You're glad you're in co-ed school, in fact?

BOY: (with real depth of feeling) Oh yes sir!

MB: Why do you say it with such heartfelt feeling?

BOY: You see, the boys at the secondary school, they sort of think it's an achievement to get the cane, sir: it seems an entirely different attitude to schooling, sir.

MB: But what has this to do with boys and girls?

BOY: It's a single sex school and it has a much stricter atmosphere and I don't think you can learn so well in that atmosphere.

The list of the fourth year topics from Scarcombe girls' grammar school gives no indication of a feminine bias when compared with the list from the boys' school; but the girls from Daymer did give the impression that there are certain aspects which appeal particularly to girls. The list includes on the credit side 'Education in the nineteenth century', 'Elizabeth Fry', 'Shaftesbury': on the debit side 'trade unions' (obviously very unpopular) and 'mines and factory acts'. When asked about the topics she disliked, a girl from Daymer said: 'Things that don't concern us as girls.'

MB: Such as?

GIRL: Trade unions and things like that.

MB: You might become a trade unionist, mightn't you?

GIRL: You might – but there's not much possibility.

One Daymer girl's explanation of her enjoyment of the topics 'Shaftesbury', 'Fry' and 'the French Revolution' is particularly feminine.

'I enjoyed Lord Shaftesbury and Elizabeth Fry because they did everything possible to help the poor, children, criminals and those badly off. I enjoyed the French revolution because the ordinary people stood up for what they believed in, also they wanted the terrible conditions improved.'

Girls perhaps are more directly interested in the human element in history than boys: this was something which the interviews and their interest in biographies seemed to show. Time and again the girls would reply in this vein when asked what topics they enjoyed:

'Learning about different people and the work they've done. The monarchy . . . I think just people in history in general' (D G S).

'I like it better with people than politics' (Girl, B G S).

'I like hearing about individuals and their influence on government' (S G S);

and they usually made it clear that individuals rather than people in the mass were what interested them most. This is perhaps nothing more than an indication of the maternal instinct – the woman's concern for particular people, particular motives. Boys are no less interested in what is loosely called social history; but their interest is broader and more robust, and less inclined to linger over the minutiae of human behaviour.

Though perhaps military topics are more popular with younger boys (the pre-'O' level topic choices indicate this), it would seem that by the fourth year detailed choice of material for both boys and girls is usually of secondary importance. The somewhat obvious and overriding impression is that for the pupils treatment of the topic rather than the topic itself is what really matters.

CONCLUSIONS AND RECOMMENDATIONS

It might seem that the principal conclusion which can be drawn from the above two sections is that 'methods are more important than material' or that 'we should teach what history we like so long as we interest the pupils'. Such statements put the cart before the horse, for teaching techniques are a means to an end – the acquisition of knowledge, skills and attitudes by the pupils; and though the children may be more concerned with classroom activity than syllabus content, the teacher must start with a clear programme of the history he wishes to teach. The programme will lie within the broad syllabus framework, a framework shaped by the philosophy which forms the basis of the history course. This philosophy is more often implicit than explicit; and certainly the discussions with the senior history teachers seemed to indicate that there are certain pressures rather than clear cut principles which help to form the outline of the syllabus, a climate of opinion to which the five teachers consciously or unconsciously have responded.

Such conventions can be seen behind the chronological framework within which the syllabuses have been set. The framework assumes that history in the secondary school must start with 'early man' and progress chronologically so that by the fifth year, when the majority will discontinue the study of history, the end of the nineteenth, perhaps the early twentieth, century has been reached. This developmental or 'span of history' approach is a product of the English nineteenth-century educational system, which was dominated by the fee-paying schools and the ancient universities. It was felt that those who were destined to occupy influential positions at home and in the empire should be given a sound knowledge of the development of the British constitution; and public school history reflected this requirement by concentrating on the British kings and queens, and the story of the evolution of parliament and the legal system. The state schools adopted a pale imitation of this syllabus taught to the future leaders of England. History at the elementary and secondary levels was essentially developmental, and was intended to give pupils a healthy respect for British institutions; the spirit of Macaulay and the other Whig historians still brooded over the scene.

The doubts which the Great War cast served to modify the syllabus. Constitutional history gave way to a little social history (G. G. Coulton's influence was important here). In certain schools more emphasis was put on the history of Europe. Some were adventurous enough to include American history. Lines of development – transport, dress, housing through the ages – were studied by the 'less able', 'patches' by others. The framework, however, within which these modifications were contained remained unchanged. Pupils grew up with history; the major events of 'our island story' had to be covered; continuity and direction could only be given through a strictly chronological approach.[1]

This is the tradition which has helped to shape the syllabuses of the five schools. With Neil and Scarcombe the influence is less apparent, for they have modified the conventional syllabus to include topics from 'world history', and certainly the chronological framework has largely been abandoned in their first year courses (though it must be remembered that the boys from Neil who took part in this investigation had been studying a 'normal' English history course – cave men to 1914 in five years). The syllabuses of Benborough, Daymer and Fairport, however, have all been placed firmly within an outline framework, which covers the traditional aspects of British history and takes the story more or less chronologically up to the present century.

The more detailed selection of material for topics within the syllabus framework seems to be determined by three factors. First, the interests of the teacher; secondly, the interests and abilities of the pupils; thirdly, in the fourth and fifth years, the requirements of the external examinations. It would seem that the first two factors present few complications and lead to a satisfactory selection of material; the third factor tends to restrict the form and content of history teaching. It is, however, doubtful whether the 'span of history' approach which embraces these criteria provides a valid philosophy for the teaching of school history.

The arguments against the traditional framework are twofold. First,

[1] See M. E. Bryant, 'Trends in history teaching', *Didaskalos*, vol. 1, no. 3, 1965 pp. 92–103.

research other than mine has shown that it is not until the mental age of about fifteen that most children acquire an historical time sense.[1] This can be defined as the ability to view history as an 'ever-changing pattern of events which are, as it were, ripples on the stream of time'; the capacity to see the past as an unfolding story in which events are placed in time relation to each other. Such maturity of outlook is seldom achieved by the young adolescent; and developmental syllabuses that seem cohesive and logical to the adult will probably appear illogical and fragmented to most pupils in the junior and middle forms of the secondary school because they have not acquired the time perspective with which to bind the periods together. 'Fifty years or five thousand' as Mr Neville said, 'It's all the same to boys'; and the other teachers (with the exception of Mr Freeman) made it clear that they do not expect their pupils to acquire an historical time sense before the sixth form. The evidence obtained from the time questions in the history tests used for this investigation[2] tends to confirm these opinions. The answers indicate that many of the boys and, in particular, the girls, are unsure of this aspect of history. If this is true of selected pupils, what must the position be like with the less able?

Secondly, not only does the developmental or outline syllabus tend to give pupils little sense of continuity but it encourages superficial coverage: as one pupil said, 'What we do is the sort of top layer of history'. This remark is substantiated in general by the analysis of the completed research history tests. Many of the pupils' answers indicated that their knowledge is superficial and unstructured; that topics seldom made an impact and were often considered as discrete pieces of information with all the implications of externality that this implies.

The enquiry has produced enough evidence to show how justified are the critics of the outlines syllabuses; it is clear that the attempt to give a continuous, overall picture of the span of history embracing the traditional English events should be abandoned. Yet what should replace the old order? Writers such as Mr Carpenter argue strongly in favour of a syllabus composed of patches or 'eras' – studies in depth of small periods of history;[3] others such as Professor Jeffreys[4] recommend lines of development. While both approaches to a certain extent are answers to the deficiencies of the outline course, neither are historically or philosophically entirely satisfactory, for they tend to limit the scope and content of the teaching. Instead, it has been argued[5] that 'themes' should be taken for each year group – that is, important and relevant problems in history. Each theme should form a logical unit; between years, however, there will not necessarily be chronological continuity. The theme is more flexible than

[1] See G. Jahoda, 'Children's concepts of time and history', *Educational Review*, vol. 15, 1963, pp. 87–104.
[2] Paper I, numbers 1A, 1B, 2 and 3 (see App. VI, p. 171).
[3] P. Carpenter, *History: the Era Approach*, Cambridge University Press, 1964.
[4] M. V. C. Jeffreys, *History in Schools: the study of development*, Pitman, 1948.
[5] For example, Miss M. E. Bryant in a lecture entitled 'The history syllabus reconsidered', given to the Historical Association on 6 January 1967.

the patch in that it is not limited to a particular time period; it is historically more acceptable than the line of development in that it embraces a wider spectrum of human activity. It combines the advantages of both by requiring a fairly intensive study in depth; and, like the patch or line of development syllabus, the study of themes makes no pretence at giving total coverage.

The second major change to the traditional syllabus concerns recent and world history. The majority of the pupils felt that these aspects of history are relevant and important; and the introduction of themes from recent and world history might well be a way of maintaining interest at a stage when pupils often begin to turn against the subject. Such a change is not advocated on the grounds of pupil preference alone. Four of the five teachers felt that British history is no longer adequate for tomorrow's citizens, and that the secondary school course must adopt a more cosmopolitan outlook. Many of the answers to the world history questions in the research history tests reinforce this argument by indicating the pupils' anglocentric outlook. Indeed, the teachers' attitudes are symptomatic of a growing feeling that most secondary school history syllabuses are too limited in their scope; and the Department of Education's recent pamphlet *Towards World History* highlights and emphasises the need to broaden the course and select topics according to their relevance to the modern world.

Four criteria therefore are suggested for the construction of a syllabus.
1. The 'span of history' approach should be abandoned and 'themes' adopted.
2. These themes should fulfil today's need for a world rather than a European outlook.
3. For the final year or years of the course, the themes should be taken from the twentieth century.
4. The teacher's interests should determine the detailed selection of material, having due regard to the interests and abilities of the pupils.

These criteria underline the essential practice of good history teaching: the interaction between the teacher, material and pupil. They presuppose a general framework which the particular requirements of the pupils amplify and adjust.

It is perhaps unwise to suggest a course based on these criteria, for their application permits wide variation. However, some indication must be given of the possible form of a five year secondary school syllabus. It must be emphasised that what follows has been drawn up partly with the writer's own (comprehensive) school in mind; and though the ideas stem from the investigation, the syllabus is designed for a wide range of abilities. It rests on the assumption that all pupils will take history for two periods a week until the end of the third year, and that it then becomes an optional examination subject taken for four periods a week. The fourth and fifth year course could form the basis of a mode 2 or 3 C S E (or G C E) syllabus. No mention is made of local studies, mainly because this is such a personal and particular matter. It is assumed that local history will be studied in its own right or to illustrate an aspect of the main syllabus as and when the class teacher thinks fit. Examples of the way in which it could be included are given at the end of the next chapter (on teaching techniques). One final point: to give a syllabus without suggesting suitable books would be wrong, and at the end of each year's course a short list of books has been appended. The assumption here is that the issue of an outline textbook for a year's work is abandoned and that the department will concentrate on a collection of 'pools' of books readily available for class and home work so that as far as possible pupils are encouraged to consult different 'authorities'. The bibliographies have been drawn up with this in mind. Most of the series listed are still expanding; but apart from books in active preparation details of projected titles are not given. The exception is a modern history series planned by Faber, the first titles of which should be on the market in 1968. Those who want more information will of course turn to the invaluable *Handbook for History Teachers* edited by W. H. Burston and C.W. Green (Methuen, 1962), which gives, amongst other information, a comprehensive bibliography of books for use in school. Some local authorities, too (such as Kent), publish lists of recommended books. Information about historical fiction can be obtained from the *Handbook*, and from two Historical Association pamphlets: K. Charlton, *Recent Historical Fiction for Secondary School Children* (11 – 15 years) (Teaching of History leaflet No. 18, 1960) and H. Cam, *Historical Novels* (G.48, 1961).

Many teachers will want to inspect the books listed with the syllabus. School books are seldom displayed in shops; but those teachers who are in the London area can visit the National Reference Textbook Library at the London Institute of Education, Malet Street, London W.C.1. The Historical Association has a textbook library at its headquarters, 59A, Kennington Park Road, London S.E.11. However, many institutes and schools of education (as well as local authorities – notably Manchester and the Inner London authority) have collections of textbooks, and teachers in other areas no doubt could obtain advice and help from the librarians. Colleges of education, too, may have collections which teachers might be allowed to inspect. Finally, it is worth mentioning the children's sections of public libraries which often contain a varied and useful assortment of historical reference books and fiction.

First year

The first year syllabus lays the foundations for the following years by dealing with the early civilisations (including those of the Far East), the Graeco-Roman world and, in the third term, aspects of the medieval world. Such topics can be made of absorbing interest to eleven-year-olds; a great many of the pupils who took part in this investigation seemed to have enjoyed these periods of history.

The first year syllabus as it stands contains too many topics to be covered in the year; and fairly rigorous selection will have to be made. For example, in the first term theme, topics from two of the four areas (including one from the Far East) could be taken.

Term one theme
ORIGINS: CIVILISATION IN THE MIDDLE AND FAR EAST

Select topics from two of the following four areas, including one from the Far East.

1. The Fertile Crescent
Geographical setting: the importance of the Tigris and Euphrates.
The Sumerians. The early settlers: pottery, weaving, farming, use of stone. The arch and the wheel. The Flood. Third dynasty at Ur: houses; clothing; slavery; cuneiform writing; trade.
Babylon. Hammurabi; the laws. The Assyrians and the fall of Babylon. Nineveh. Nebuchadnezzar and the New Babylon.
The Hebrews. Abraham, 'father of multitudes' and monotheism. Kings. Roman occupation and destruction of the Hebrews in Palestine. Contributions of Jews to Western civilisation.

2. Egypt
Geographical setting: the Nile valley.
Lower and Upper Egypt: the union.
The pyramid builders; the middle kingdom; the empire (with particular reference to Akenaten, Nefertiti and Tutankhamen).
Life in Egypt: rulers and workers; craftsmen; homes; temples and religion; writing.
Egypt today – through films, pictures and so on.

3. India
Geographical setting: the Indus valley.
Brunton and Cunningham; the discovery of Harappa and Mohenjodaro.
Climatic conditions: pre-Aryan civilisation. The Aryan invasion. Aryan wheeled carts, horses. Aryan language, religion. Aryans as rulers, lawyers, soldiers, priests (cf. Norman Conquest of Britain).
Brahmins and class divisions.
The life of Buddha; importance of Buddhism today.
Alexander the Great and the Invasion of India: the battle of Hydaspes, 326 B C, Europe and India face to face.
India today – through films, pictures and so on.

4. China
Geographical setting.
Origins; the Shang and Chou dynasties, 1027 – 250 B C.
Shaping of the Chinese empire under Chi'in dynasty, 221 – 206 B C.

Building of the Great Wall.

Creation of a common language.

Teaching of Confucius; stratification of society.

Transport and communications; homes and living conditions.

Han dynasty, 206 B C – A D 209. Expansion of the empire: the arrival of Buddhism. Art; science.

Marco Polo; East meets West.

Reasons for the decline of China's civilisation.

China today: the emergence of new world power – through films, pictures, and so on.

Term two theme

THE GLORY THAT WAS GREECE AND THE GRANDEUR THAT WAS ROME: THE FOUNDATIONS OF WESTERN CIVILISATION

1. Greece

Geographical setting: the Aegean bridge. Crete and Knossus.

Greek occupation of the Peloponnese.

The City State: Persian wars and the rise of Athens.

Democracy; religion and philosophy; the Greek alphabet; art and architecture; stories from the Illiad and Odyssey; Greek plays; the Olympic games; farming and trade.

Contrasts between the city states: Sparta and Athens.

Peloponnesian wars; Pericles; Plato and Socrates; Alexander the Great; the decline of Greece.

2. Rome

Geographical setting. Origins. Kings. The establishment of the Republic.

The struggles with Hannibal.

Julius Ceasar. The establishment of the empire. Government; religion; the arts; daily life in Rome. Roman armies and warfare.

The expansion of the empire: the conquest of Britain.

A Roman town in Britain (e.g. Silchester); Roman roads; Roman baths; Roman villas.

The empire and Christianity.

The fall of the empire.

Importance of Graeco-Roman contributions to Western civilisation.

Italy and Greece today – through films, pictures and so on.

Term three theme

THE STRUCTURE OF WESTERN SOCIETY IN THE HIGH MIDDLE AGES

1. Feudalism

The 'noble savage'; tribal society; the origins of feudalism on the European continent.

Feudalism comes to Britain. The Domesday book. The feudal oath; duties of the feudal lord. Castles and warfare. Feudal justice.
The manorial system.
The breakdown of the feudal system; extension of the king's peace; growth of the parliamentary system; growth of towns and guilds.

2. The Christian Church

The village church and church architecture.
Monasticism.
The mendicant orders (through, e.g., life of St Francis).
The Jesuits (through life of St Ignatius Loyola).
The inquisition.
Medieval ecclesiastical art.
The church and science.

3. The Cross and the Crescent

Mohammedanism (through life of Mohammed).
Clashes between Christians and Moslems: Spain; the crusades.
Arab universities in Spain; contributions of Arabs to Western knowledge (science, mathematics, medicine, writing, art).

First Year Bibliography

CHATTO AND WINDUS

Dawn of History Series, R. Carrington
Ancient Eypt, 1959; *Ancient Sumer*, 1959; *Ancient Greece*, 1961; *Ancient Rome*, 1961.

EVANS

Visual History Series
A Visual History of India, A. B. Jeffries, 1966
A Visual History of China, A. B. Jeffries, 1966

GINN

Museum Bookshelf Series, editor: C. B. Firth
Ancient Civilizations (First Shelf), A. F. Titterton and K. M. Gadd, 1958 (The Bronze Age and Early Iron Age; Everyday Life in Sumer and Babylonia; Work and Play in Ancient Egypt; The Warfare and Hunting of Assyrian Kings; The Arts of Greece)

History Bookshelf Series, editor: C. B. Firth
The Middle Ages (Green Shelf), A. F. Titterton, 1954 (Bayeux Tapestry; English Castles; English Monasteries; Life in a Manor House; A Port and a Pilgrim; Work on a Manor)

HULTON

Ancient China, C. A. Burland, 1960; *Ancient Greece*, C. A. Burland, 1958; *Ancient Rome*, C. A. Burland, 1958

LONGMANS

Evidence in Pictures Series, Islay Doncaster
The Roman Occupation of Britain, 1961
The Medieval Church, 1961

The World Before Britain, E. H. Dance, second edition 1965

Then and There Series, editor: M. E. Reeves.
Ancient Egypt, E. J. Sheppard, 1960
Ancient Crete and Mycenae, J. Bolton, 1957
Ancient Athens, E. J. Sheppard, 1967
Alexander the Great, Naomi Mitchison, 1964
Ancient Rome, N. Sherwin-White, 1959
Roman Britain, Joan Liversidge, 1958
The Romans in Scotland, O. Thomson, 1967
The Norman Conquest, M. E. Reeves, 1959
Medieval Pilgrimages, Gladys Scott Thomson, 1962
The Medieval Village, M. E. Reeves, 1954
The Medieval Town, M. E. Reeves, 1953
The Medieval Feast, R. J. Mitchell, 1958
The Medieval Castle, M. E. Reeves, 1958
The Medieval Monastery, M. E. Reeves, 1963
The Medieval Tournament, R. J. Mitchell, 1958
Wool Merchants of the Fifteenth Century, Gladys Scott Thomson, 1958

MACMILLAN

Sources of History Series.
Archery in the Middle Ages, E. K. Milliken, 1967

MAX PARISH AND OLDBOURNE

They Lived Like This Series. Isotype Institute
. . . *in Ancient Mesopotomia*, Marie Neurath and Evelyn Worboys, 1964
. . . *in Ancient Egypt*, Marie Neurath and John Ellis, 1965
. . . *in Ancient Palestine*, Marie Neurath and Evelyn Worboys, 1965
. . . *in Ancient Crete*, Marie Neurath and John Ellis, 1964
. . *in Ancient China*, Marie Neurath and Evelyn Worboys, 1966

METHUEN

Outline Series
Crusades, R. R. Sellman, 1955

36

OXFORD UNIVERSITY PRESS

People of the Past Series, general editor: Phillipa Pearce
A Soldier on Hadrian's Wall, Duncan Taylor, 1962
A Romano-British Family, Vera White, 1962
A Thirteenth Century Villein, Patience Andrewes, 1964
A Fifteenth Century Wool Merchant, Cynthia Harnett, 1962
An Archer in the Army of Edward III, Michael Blakeway, 1962
A Fifteenth Century London Housewife, Francis Makover, 1965
An Eleventh Century Mason, Joan Pager, 1966
A Twelfth Century Nun, Catherine Northcote, 1966

WEIDENFELD AND NICOLSON

Pathfinder Biographies, editor: E. Royston Pike
Mohammed, E. Royston Pike, 1962

Young Historian Series, editor: C. Green
Ancient China, Cornelia Spencer, 1963
Ancient India, E. Royston Pike, 1961
Ancient Egypt, Roger Lancelyn Green, 1963
Lands of the Bible, E. Royston Pike, 1962
Ancient Greece, Roger Lancelyn Green, 1962
Republican Rome, E. Royston Pike, 1966
Imperial Rome, H. E. L. Mellersh, 1965

Second Year

The theme here is the developing awareness of Europeans as they come into contact with new knowledge, new peoples. The history of this period is particularly exciting and colourful, and there should be no difficulty in finding visual and documentary material. Many of the themes should be taken through to the nineteenth or twentieth centuries.

Term one theme

RENAISSANCE AND REFORMATION

1. Europe in the Fifteenth Century
Society and wealth. Limited knowledge of the outside world. Trade centred in and between the Mediterranean and Baltic. Restricting effects of Ming dynasty in China (who cut contacts with the West), Ottoman Turks and Black Death.

2. The Renaissance
Italy in the fifteenth century. The City States. Wealth and importance of Venice, Genoa, Florence. Italy the centre of 'world' trade.
The Renaissance seen in art; sculpture; architecture; writing. The

Renaissance studied through individuals, e.g. Leonardo de Vinci; Michelangelo; Galileo; Bramante; Erasmus; Sir Thomas More.
The Renaissance and education.
The spread of the Renaissance to Germany, France, England.

3. The Reformation

Martin Luther; life and beliefs. The Lutheran church in Scandinavia, on the continent.
John Calvin; life and beliefs. Effects of Calvinism on the continent and the world (e.g. in Massachusetts, in South Africa.)
Henry VIII and the political reformation in England. Dissolution of the monasteries. Protestantism under Edward VI and Elizabeth.

Term two theme
THE JOURNEY INTO THE UNKNOWN: THE VOYAGES AND EXPEDITIONS OF DISCOVERY

1. Geographical knowledge in the fourteenth century: seamen, ships, charts, instruments fourteenth to sixteenth century

2. The voyages and expeditions of discovery

a. Trade with the East: incentives to find a sea route.
   Portugal: reasons for Portugal taking the lead. Prince Henry the Navigator. Bartholomew Diaz. Vasco da Gama.
   Spain: Columbus and Magellan
   England and France: the search for the Northern passages. The Cabots; Cartier.
b. Later voyages and expeditions.
   Dampier, Cook and the opening up of Australia.
   Exploration in Africa, nineteenth century.
   Exploration in the Arctic and Antarctic.

3. Colonisation by European powers

a. The Spanish Conquistadores and America: Cortes and the Aztecs; Pizarro and the Incas.
   Britain and North America: New England; the Plantations.
   Trading depots in the East.
b. Later expansion of British influence in India.
   Penal settlements in Australia.
   Nineteenth-century colonisation in the Far East: e.g. French Indo-China; English Singapore and Hongkong.
   Nineteenth-century colonisation of Africa.

4. European reaction to and treatment of the outside world
Jesuits and their missionary efforts.

American colonists and the Indians; Canadian colonists and the Indians. The Slave trade.

Term three theme
CLASHES OVER THE DIVISION OF SPOILS: GREAT POWER RIVALRY

1. Trade and trading companies
Objectives and organisation. The companies in operation, through specific examples, e.g. the English East India Company; the Dutch East India company under Coen and Van Diemen.

2. English and Spanish rivalry in the sixteenth century
The Spanish empire and the greatness of Spain.
The decline of Spain: the Spanish armada.

3. Portugese, English and Dutch rivalry in the sixteenth and seventeenth centuries
The rise of the United Provinces as a trading and banking nation.
Dutch greatness seen in art and architecture.
The Dutch and Portugese in the Far East.
Britain and the Dutch; the seventeenth-century trade wars.
The decline of the United Provinces.

4. English and French rivalry in the eighteenth century
Background: the France of Louis XIV. St Simon at Versailles.
Treatment mainly through the Seven Years War – with particular reference to Canada, India, the war at sea.
End with Trafalgar: Britain rules the waves?

Second year bibliography

CHATTO AND WINDUS

Studies in English History Series, G. R. Kesteven
The Reformation in England, 1965; *The Armada*, 1965; *The Mayflower Pilgrims*, 1966

FABER

The Story of Michaelangelo, Agnes Allen, 1953
Sir Francis Drake, Christopher Lloyd, 1957

GINN

History Bookshelf Series, editor: C. B. Firth
Under Tudor Rulers (Yellow shelf), C. B. Firth, 1965 (Bible and Prayer Books; Elizabethan Houses; Elizabethan Playtime; Elizabethan Schools and Schoolboys; Girls at Home; Ships and Seamen).

The Age of the Stuarts (Red shelf), F. Armytage, 1966 (A Village in the Civil War; Sunday; Witches, Astrologers, Men of Learning; Plague in Town and Village; A Planter in the New World; Adventure to the East)

LONGMANS

Evidence in Pictures Series, Islay Doncaster
Elizabethan and Jacobean Home Life, 1960

The Expansion of Europe, Patrick Richardson, 1966

Then and There Series, editor: M. E. Reeves
Henry Percy and Henry VIII, Kathleen Davis, 1967
Elizabethan Citizen, M. E. Reeves and P. Hodgson, 1961
The Elizabethan Ship, Gregory Robinson, 1956
Elizabethan Court, M. E. Reeves, 1956
The Elizabethan Village, A. J. Fletcher, 1967
Plymouth Ho! The West in Elizabethan Times, Patricia Donahue, 1958
Captain John Smith and Virginia, W. J. C. Gill, 1967
The Pilgrim Fathers, W. J. C. Gill, 1964
Richard Baxter: Toleration and Tyranny, (1615–1691), Katherine Moore, 1964
John Newton and the Slave Trade, Bernard Martin, 1961
Clive in India, D. W. Sylvester, 1967
Glasgow and the Tobacco Lords, Norman Nichol, 1966
The Struggle for Canada, B. Williams, 1967
Nelson's Navy, P. Richardson, 1967

OXFORD UNIVERSITY PRESS

Lives of Great Men and Women Series, Norman Wymer
Great Explorers, 1956 (Columbus; Magellan; Cook; Mackenzie; Franklin; Livingstone; Scott; Hunt)
Soldiers and Sailors, 1960 (Drake; Marlborough; Wolfe; Wellington; Nelson; Gordon; Clive; Alanbrooke)

People of the Past Series, general editor: Phillipa Pearce
An Elizabethan Actor, John Allen, 1962
An Elizabethan Sailor, E. J. Boog-Watson, 1964
An Elizabethan Lady of the Manor, Hazel Richardson, 1962
A Settler in New England, Leonard F. James, 1966
A Puritan Preacher, J. R. Batten, 1964
A Seaman at the Time of Trafalgar, Hester Burton, 1963
An Australian Settler, Mary Durack, 1964

WEIDENFELD AND NICOLSON

Pathfinder Biographies, editor: E. Royston Pike
Leonardo da Vinci, Ivor B. Hart, 1964

Young Historian Series, editor: C. Green
The Reformation, Leonard Cowie, 1967
The Renaissance, George Bull, 1968

Third year

The course starts by comparing the development of British local and national government with the development in other parts of the world. Scientific, technological and medical progress is explored in the second term; and in the third the course is brought up to date by contrasting these achievements with the divisions and problems of today's world.

Term one theme
GOVERNMENT

1. 1775 and 1789
Two revolutions to illustrate the violent reorganisation of society and government in America and France.

2. Britain after Waterloo: the 'peaceful' revolution
The establishment of a police force.
Parliament: the unreformed House of Commons; extension of the franchise.
Paternalism in government.
Growth of towns and extension of powers of Local Authorities.
Extension of education.
The growth of the welfare state.
Party government.

3. Contrasts: the world in 1914
Life and government in Italy, America, Russia, China.

Term two theme
SCIENCE, TECHNOLOGY AND INDUSTRY

1. The overthrow of Aristotelian science

2. Newtonian science

3. Theory and practice – through topics
For example:
a. Mining and metallurgy: the age of iron and steel.
　Development in Britain. Abraham Darby. Growing production: importance in Britain's development. Challenge from Germany. Production in America. Position today.
b. Roads.
　Roman road building (recap). Medieval roads; pilgrimages; packhorses; turnpike trusts. Macadam, Metcalfe, Telford. Coaches and

coaching inns. Railways and effects on roads. The motor car and effects on roads. Military road building in twentieth-century Germany. Roads in America. British roads today: the Buchanan report.

c. Canals.

River navigation. Continental canals in the seventeenth century. Canal building in England in the eighteenth century. Duke of Bridgewater. Effects of canal building on industry. Decline of canals with coming of railways.

Suez canal; Panama canal; Kiel canal.

d. Railways.

Development of steam power through to the railway age: emphasis on the 'great names'. Establishment of a railway system in England. Effect on trade; way of life; law and order.

Railway system on the Continent; in the Americas; in China.

Position in England today; Beeching axe. Steam to diesel.

e. Internal combustion engine.

Work of Marcus, Benz and Daimler in Germany.

Panhard, Levassor in France.

Henry Ford in America.

Early opposition in England.

Effect of the motor car on industry, way of life.

Motor car manufacture in Japan, Russia, China.

The jet engine.

Internal combustion engine in warfare.

f. Electricity.

Early history. Development of the dynamo.

Application of electricity to industry. Electricity and domestic use.

Hydro-electric power: Scotland, Egypt, Canada, U.S.A.

g. Radio.

Life of Marconi.

Radio in peace and war.

4. Medical science

Early history: magic and superstition.

Greek medicine: Dark Ages and epidemics.

Development: seventeenth century, Harvey; eighteenth century, Jenner and small pox.

The conquest of pain. Florence Nightingale and nursing reforms.

Lister and antiseptics. Public health in the nineteenth century.

Developments in the twentieth century: X-rays, radium, penicillin.

The N.H.S.

The Red Cross.

The W.H.O.

World population and birth control.

5. Evolution
Darwin and the origin of species – through the voyage of the *Beagle*.
The 'challenge' to religious belief.

6. Nuclear physics: the power for good and evil
Early history: the splitting of the atom.
The first atom bombs: Hiroshima and Nagasaki.
Proliferation of nuclear weapons: the East-West confrontation over Cuba.
Test ban treaties.
Atoms for peace (e.g. Calder Hall). EURATOM.

Term three theme
THE WORLD TODAY

1. Contrasts between the underdeveloped and developed countries
Income per head; food production; industrial development; education.
A general survey followed by a particular study, e.g. India and Britain.
Desperate need for co-operation.

2. Barriers to co-operation
Racialism in Africa, U.S.A., Britain, Germany.
Religious intolerance.
Political differences between East and West.

3. Attempts at co-operation
e.g. through Commonwealth; United Nations Organisation; aid from America, Russia, Britain to underdeveloped countries; Voluntary Service Overseas.

Third year bibliography

BLOND EDUCATIONAL

Today is History Series, general editor: C. E. Stuart-Jervis.
Strike or Bargain? The story of Trades Unionism, D. J. Williams, 1964
Crime and Society, Ben Whitaker, 1964
I Swear and Vow: The Story of Medicine, Eric J. Trimmer, 1966
The Monarchy, Roger Lockyer, 1965
The Press, Brian Inglis, 1964
The Wage Packet: How the Economy Works, P. Hanson, 1965

FABER

Humphrey Davy: 'Pilot' of Penzance, James Kendall, 1954
Michael Faraday: Man of Simplicity, James Kendall, 1955

Men and Events Series, general editor: A. F. Alington
The Man Who Discovered Penicillin: a Life of Sir Alexander Fleming,
W. A. C. Bullock, 1963
Marconi and the Discovery of Wireless, Leslie Reade, 1963

GINN

History Bookshelf Series, editor: C. B. Firth
Georgian England (Orange Shelf), F. Armytage, 1962, (Life in a Country
House; Life in a Manufacturing Town; Roads and Waterways; Sailors
and Ships; Life in a Village; A Trip to a Watering Place).
Onward from Victoria (Grey Shelf), A. F. Titterton, 1965, (Ships in
Peace and War; The Soldier and the Airman; From Place to Place; The
Fight for Health; Sport and Leisure; Changes in Domestic Life).

LONGMANS

Evidence in Pictures Series, Islay Doncaster
Social Conditions in England 1760–1830, 1964
Changing Society in Victorian England, 1850–1900, 1966

Modern Times Series
The Making of the Welfare State, R. H. Cootes, 1966 with 7″ L P record

Then and There Series, editor: M. E. Reeves
Roads and Canals in the Eighteenth Century, Marjorie Greenwood, 1953
The American Revolution, Clorinda Clarke, 1964
The French Revolution, M. Rosenthal, 1965
Parliamentary Elections and Reforms 1807–1832, John Addy, 1961
London Life and the Great Exhibition of 1851, J. R. C. Yglesias, 1964
The Motor Revolution, David St. J. Thomas, 1961
Police and Prisons, P. F. Speed, 1967
The Chartists, P. Searby, 1967
Edwardian England, A. Delgado, 1967
The Railway Revolution, Majorie Greenwood, 1955

MACMILLAN

Sources of History Series
The English Poor Law, J. J. and A. J. Bagley, 1966
Parliamentary Reform, J. W. Derry, 1966
Chartism, Christopher Thorne, 1966
Development of Power, O. Ashmore, 1967
Emergence of a Scientific Society, G. Roderick, 1967

OXFORD UNIVERSITY PRESS

Lives of Great Men and Women Series, Norman Wymer
Social Reformers, 1955 (Arnold of Rugby; Elizabeth Fry; Hill; Peel;
Robert Owen; Barnardo; Florence Nightingale; Shaftesbury)

Great Inventors, 1957 (Watt; Stephenson; Braille; Bessemer; Daimler; Edison; Marconi; Wright Brothers)
Medical Scientists and Doctors, 1958 (Marie Curie; Pasteur; Elizabeth Garret Anderson; Harvey; Pavlov; Lister; Schweitzer; Fleming)

People of the Past Series, general editor: Phillipa Pearce
An Eighteenth Century Toll-Keeper, Rosaleen Whately, 1962
A Canal Builder, Michael Blakeway, 1962
A Soldier in Washington's Army, Leonard F. James, 1964
A Nurse in the Crimea, Catherine Northcote, 1966
A Nineteenth Century Lancashire Weaver's Family, W. T. Selley, 1965

WEIDENFELD AND NICOLSON

Pathfinder Biographies, editor: E. Royston Pike
James Watt, Ivor B. Hart, 1962
Michael Faraday, David Gumston, 1962
Joseph Lister, Frederick Cartwright, 1963
Karl Marx, Arnold Kettle, 1963
Charles Darwin, H. E. L. Mellersh, 1964
Marie Curie, Alan Ivimey, 1964
Marconi: Father of Radio, David Gunston 1965
Gottlieb Daimler, Anthony Bird, 1962
Ernest Rutherford, John Rowland, 1964

Fourth and fifth years

This syllabus is designed as a two year examination course. It starts with the world today; it looks at Europe in 1900 and emphasises the opportunities this wealthy and powerful area of the world had at that time; it then deals with the two world wars. This sets the scene for an examination of some of the attempts at co-operation made after 1945 and for an assessment of the problems which divide the world. The course concludes by looking at internationalism today.

The syllabus essentially is an extension of the third year, third term course of study. It owes a certain amount to a model published in the Parliamentary Group for World Government's pamphlet *History Syllabuses and the World Perspective* (1962). Inevitably there is some overlap between the sections. This could be made a strength rather than a weakness of the syllabus in that it gives the opportunity to view the same problem from a different angle.

Themes for terms one and two
A. THE WORLD TODAY: INTRODUCTION

1. Its size
Dimensions in miles and hours of travelling. Means of transport in 1700, 1850, 1960.

2. Its wealth
Natural resources; their development and exploitation.

3. Its population
World population trends over the centuries

4. Its inequality of living standards

5. Its political boundaries

B. EUROPE THE HUB OF THE WORLD IN 1900

1. Geographical and political picture of Europe in 1900
largely through map work.

2. Britain in 1900 : the heyday of the middle-classes
Population increases. Inequalities of wealth and living standards. Franchise extensions. Transport and power. Industrial position and challenge from Germany and the U S A. The Public Schools and the 'White Man's burden'. (There will be no attempt to give an overall detailed picture here. The aim will be to present some sense of the 'quality of life' of the time. The approach will be largely through project work.)

C. THE FAILURE OF INTERNATIONAL CO-OPERATION: THE FIRST WORLD WAR

1. Britain's abandonment of splendid isolation
Causes of the First World War.

2. Main stages of the war
Western Front; Middle East; War at Sea.

3. Results
Versailles: its effects on the balance of power.

D. ATTEMPTS TO KEEP INTERNATIONAL ORDER AND THEIR FAILURE, 1919–39: THE SECOND WORLD WAR

1. Formation of the League of Nations
Its structure
Locarno treaties of 1925
Germany under Stresemann and the League
Kellogg-Briand Pact of 1928

2. The challenge from
The Nazi Party (through life of Hitler)

Italian fascism (through life of Mussolini)
Japan and the warlords.

3. The breakdown of collective security
Manchuria, 1931
Abyssinia, 1935
The Rhineland, 1936
Spain, 1936
Austria and Sudetenland, 1938
Czechoslovakia and Poland, 1939

4. The main stages of the war
Early stages to 1940
Entry of the U S S R and U S A
War in the air
War at sea
War in the Far East

5. The peace

Themes for terms three and four
E. ATTEMPTS AT CO-OPERATION

1. The League of Nations and its failure (recap)

2. The United Nations Organisation
Formation: aims:
Structure and working.
Work of the U N in preserving world peace: Korea 1953; Suez 1956; The
Congo 1960; Aden 1967.
Work of U N E S C O in assisting underdeveloped countries.
Work of W H O in combating disease.
Work of F A O in combating hunger.
Work of I L O (founded 1919 – joined with U N 1946).
Work of International Court of Justice.

3. NATO: SEATO: CENTO: Warsaw Treaty Organisation

4. The Arab League

5. The European movement
Background: Charlemagne and the Holy Roman Empire; the Catholic
Church. The growth of nationalism; Napoleon; Hitler; the E E C; E F T A.

6. The Commonwealth
Background: the Durham report and the British North America Act.
Developments in the twentieth century; new members from Asia and

Africa. Economic and technical assistance to developing nations of Commonwealth.

7. Pan-African movement

F. WORLD PROBLEMS TODAY: POLITICAL, SOCIAL AND ECONOMIC CONTRASTS BETWEEN USA, USSR AND COMMUNIST CHINA

1. The U.S.A.

Background: the 'New World'. The land of the western frontier and Self Help. Immigration in the nineteenth century.
System of Government.
American prosperity and poverty in the 1920's and 30's: isolationism.
The slump.
Franklin Delano Roosevelt: presidency from 1932 to 1945. The New Deal: the abandonment of isolation.
The importance of Truman (1945–1952): America an active world power. The Marshall plan. Eisenhower and Korea. Kennedy: the Kennedy round: achievements by 1963. Johnson and Vietnam.

2. The U.S.S.R.

Background: the 'ancien regime'.
Karl Marx and Communism.
1905: the abortive revolution. The 1917 revolution: part played by Lenin.
System of government.
The rule of Stalin: the extension of Russian frontiers westwards and the establishment of satellite states.
Cold war with the West. Berlin airlift 1948-49 and the Berlin wall, 1961; Hungary 1956; Cuba 1962; Czechoslovakia 1968.
The deposition of Kruschev: reconciliation with the West?

3. China

Background: the 'ancien regime'.
Sun Yat Sen and the revolution. Chiang Kai-shek.
Mao Tse-tung. The long march; the war years; the triumph of the communists.
Contrasts between Chinese and Russian communism.
The Cold War with the U S S R

Themes for terms five and six
(work on Section G should start half way through term four)

G. WORLD PROBLEMS TODAY: COLONIALISM AND NATIONALISM

1. European colonialism
exemplified in the scramble for Africa in the nineteenth century.

2. The extent and nature of the British Empire in 1914.

3. Russian colonialism
The expansion of Muscovy, sixteenth and seventeenth centuries.
Russian ambitions in the eighteenth century.
Russia and the Far East and Eastern question, nineteenth century.
Soviet attitude to the empire it inherited: Eastern Europe and the Warsaw pact.

4. The struggle for independence
Ireland in the twentieth century.
India and Gandhi.
Hungary 1956.
The Congo 1960.
Rhodesia.

5. Africa today
Economic, political and social problems of the newly independent states. A general survey followed by a particular study of, e.g. Ghana and Nigeria.

H. WORLD PROBLEMS TODAY: RACIAL AND RELIGIOUS INTOLERANCE

1. Jews and Arabs
Jewish persecution in the past.
Nazis and Jewish persecution.
Arabs and Jews today.
Zionism and the Jewish state.

2. Hindus and Moslems
The partition of India.

3. South Africa and apartheid
Religious and economic background.
Position today.

4. The Negro in the U.S.A.
Historical background and the position today.

5. Racial and religious intolerance in Britain.

I. INTERNATIONALISM TODAY

1. The shrinking world
Communications and population movement.

2. Internationalism in the world of learning
Interspace programmes.
Scientific exchanges.
Nobel prizes.
The Atlantic College.

3. Economic internationalism: the World Bank

4. Brotherhood of man and religious teaching
Christianity.
Buddhism.
Confucianism.
The move for Christian Church unity.

5. Internationalism in the world of art
The universal appeal of art through specific examples.

6. Internationalism in the world of sport
World Cup.
Olympic Games.

Fourth and fifth year bibliography

E. ARNOLD

Britain, Europe and the World 1850–1955, D. Arnold, 1966
An Historical Atlas 1789–1962 for First Examinations, R. R. Sellman, 1963

A. AND C. BLACK

Britain in the 20th Century, R. J. Unstead, 1966

BLANDFORD

An Historical Introduction to the Twentieth Century, R. W. Harris, 1966

BLOND EDUCATIONAL

Today is History Series, general editor: C. E. Stuart-Jervis
The United Nations, Katharine Savage, 1964
From Omdurman to V.E. day: The Life Span of Sir Winston Churchill, A. M. Collin, 1964
A state of War: Europe 1939–1945, Katharine Savage, 1964
Protest, Michael O'Connor, 1964
Russia, Brian Hammond, 1967
Latin America, Simon Collier, 1967

World Outlook: 1900–1965, general editor: M. E. Bryant
The first titles in this new series were published in the Summer of 1968.
The Classwork book

The Study Books
The End of an Era, John Standen, 1968. (Queen Victoria's Jubilee of 1897)
The Unsolved Problem, Martyn Dyer, 1968. (Southern Africa)
From Warlords to Red Star, Hugh Higgins, 1968. (China in the 20th century)
Kipling and the White Man's Burden, Katherine Moore, 1968
Muckrakers to New Deal, Hugh Higgins. (American economy in the 20th century)
The Edwardians, John Standen, 1968
British Democracy in the Twentieth Century, Dennis Starkings
The Lamps Go Out, A. F. Alington. (Origins and course of the First World War)
The Russian Revolutions, David Footman
Struggle in the Deserts, Harry Browne, 1968. (The Middle East from Lawrence to Nasser)
The Embattled Peace 1919–1939, Pauline Bloncourt, 1968
After the Deluge, John Standen. (English society between the wars)
Round Table of the Twentieth Century, Martyn Dyer, 1968. (The second British Commonwealth)
Three Dictators, Sir Stephen King-Hall. (Stalin, Mussolini, Hitler)
The Second World War, Harry Browne, 1968
An Old and a Young Leader, Pauline Bloncourt. (Winston Churchill and John Kennedy)
Reconciling the World, Marion Would. (The story of Coventry Cathedral and problems of reconstructing and reconciliation of nations, churches, generations)
The Hungry World, Ann McKenzie
World Co-operation, James L. Henderson, 1968. (Attempts at union in the post-war world – U.N.O., N.A.T.O., G.A.A.T.)
Family Fortunes, Katherine Moore. (A study of family history)
At Home in the World, J. M. Cherrett, 1968. (Ecology in the 20th century)
Many Inventions and New Perspectives, Louis Bloncourt. (Technology, science, philosophy and research in the 20th century)

Europe in the Post-War World 1945–1964, R. A. Adcock, 1965

Modern Times Series. A 7 inch L P record is available for each book.
World War One, S. R. Gibbons and P. Morican, 1965

Franco and the Spanish Civil War, L. E. Snellgrove, 1965
Mussolini and Italy, C. Bayne-Jardine, 1966
Hitler and Germany, R. J. Elliott, 1966
Roosevelt and the United States, D. B. O'Callaghan, 1966
Modern China, J. C. Robottom, 1967

MACMILLAN

Sources of History Series.
Visitors to China, Keith Pratt, 1968

METHUEN

An Atlas of World Affairs, A. Boyd, 4th edn., 1964
Since 1945. Aspects of Contemporary History, ed. J. L. Henderson, 1966
World Affairs Since 1919, P. Wales, 1958
World Questions : A Study Guide, ed. J. L. Henderson, second edition 1966

OXFORD UNIVERSITY PRESS

Changing World Series.
Twentieth Century Germany, Brian Catchpole, 1965
Twentieth Century Russia, Sally Pickering, 1965
Twentieth Century France, Philip Holland, 1960
America since Independence, Joan Chandler, 1966
The Cold War, Derek Heater, 1965
Documents and Descriptions : the World since 1914, R. W. Breach, 1966

PENGUIN (PELICAN)

The Economic History of World Population, Carlo M. Cipolla, rev. edn, 1964

UNIVERSITY OF LONDON PRESS

The Story of the Twentieth Century, C. F. Strong, 1966

3 Teaching techniques and objectives

Topic selection is closely connected with topic presentation, and it is perhaps a distortion of the teaching situation to talk about methods as though they are a separate entity. Nor are methods recipes which any can follow and obtain similar results. The structure of good teaching is subtle and intangible, and very dependent on the personal attributes of both teacher and taught. Nevertheless, to a certain extent techniques of teaching can be talked about in isolation; and the arguments in favour of project work and the development of visual aids and teaching equipment in general have made many history teachers re-examine their own classroom practice. History is a peculiarly difficult subject to put across. Most of the facts of history are not directly ascertainable, and the spoken word often seems a poor substitute for the tangible objects with which other subjects are often able to deal. The history teacher has to present material which is usually abstract in such a way that it makes an impact. Here there are not only the difficulties of deciding which of a number of methods to use – individual research, group work, class discussion, exposition – but also of relating techniques to their function or purpose. We may decide to show a film or filmstrip or to use documentary evidence, but these are only ways of giving the pupils knowledge or information, or allowing them to exercise their critical faculties; they are not ends in themselves. In other words, techniques are inextricably bound up with objectives; and the methods the teacher uses will indicate what he hopes to achieve with his pupils.[1] This chapter therefore moves from a discussion of the *techniques* to a consideration of the *aims* of history classroom practice. The comments of the teachers and pupils are again dealt with in two sections; a third draws conclusions and makes recommendations.

THE TEACHERS SPEAK

In the view of four of the teachers, the two methods which retain their importance throughout the five years are exposition and questioning – in her replies to the questionnaire Miss Spender made no reference to exposition, no doubt because she considered this would imply a formal lecture method. This stress on exposition and questioning is hardly surprising, for as Miss Denton said, 'It's the main way of teaching

[1] See Professor Hirst's chapter in *Studies of Education*, ed. J. W. Tibble, Routledge & Kegan Paul, 1966.

53

anything, I should have thought. After all, it's human communication between person and person.'

The textbook, however, can play its part in giving the pupils information, and the teachers discussed the use they make of it. Mr Black emphasised the increasing importance of the text book in the third, fourth and fifth years, 'partly because of the demands of the exams (we all know that) and partly, if you have a good textbook, you can increase their dependence on it and decrease the amount of notetaking they do'. For Miss Denton the textbook holds an 'important' position throughout the five years; Mr Neville considers it 'very important'. Mr Freeman indicated that the textbook is 'moderately important' in the junior and middle-schools; and feels the occasional 'ten question test' on a chapter set for homework has a part to play – a practice which Miss Denton and Mr Neville also follow, Mr Black in the first year only. Mr Freeman went on to stress something which is never popular with pupils.

'I do feel one of the things we've got to put over at all levels is the necessity of concentration in reading. . . . You set a reading prep to boys and you know perfectly well this is what he does: he does his French translation – writes that out – and then he does his maths; and then he switches on the telly and his father says "Have you done your homework?" and he replies "I've just got a bit of history reading. I'll do that in bed or on the bus going to school." One's got to try to resist that; and you've got to make them realise that it's necessary at times (not always of course) to read really thoroughly – to know everything, check everything. That's not the only sort of reading. It's also necessary for them later to get into a sort of skimming mode of reading. Nevertheless in the early stages one's got to encourage and make them be really conscientious in this way – and this is the service I think of the short answer test.'

On the other hand Miss Spender said: 'We don't stress the textbook, and I think what we've tended to do here is to get them to look at as many different books as they possibly can. The first years constantly do this. They come along with books they've brought from home. There's not a great deal of reliance placed on "The Book".' Asked about her questionnaire reply that she never used textbooks for tests she sounded incredulous. 'It never occurred to me to use them for testing. You mean giving a chapter to read and then setting questions on it? It hadn't occurred to me.'

Such spoken and written information is often condensed by the pupils into note form; for it is usually accepted that the précising of historical material in this manner is a convenient and easy way of accumulating data. All five teachers considered that notes have a part to play with each year group; but all were equally outspoken against notes which are dictated or copied from the blackboard. They expect pupils to make their own notes either from the textbook with headings suggested by the teacher or during the class as the teacher is explaining some particular topic. Duplicated notes which are handed out seem to receive little support from any of them, though sheets of notes are occasionally given to the girls at Scarcombe.

No history teacher, however, believes that lessons should consist only of talk, textbooks and note taking; and in an attempt to distinguish between this sort of work and other forms of activity the teachers were asked what they considered the balance should be between 'passive receptivity' and 'independent activity'. The former phrase, it was quickly realised, involved a particularly unhappy choice of words. Mr Freeman commented on it. 'I really rather dislike the phrase "passive receptivity". I should have thought that receptivity could never be passive'; and Mr Neville said: 'Ideally there should be no passive receptivity. The learning process, in fact, *cannot* be passive.' But the teachers realised what the somewhat clumsy and contradictory wording was trying to probe. Miss Spender replied with characteristic enthusiasm:

'Oh, mostly independent activity. If you want me to give the percentages of course I couldn't. I'm sure that half the time one's talked at one's not listening, not properly. If you're giving out you're never absolutely certain that you're giving them things they want to know. If you can teach by making them ask questions they will learn at their own rate. If they're asking the questions they're learning the sorts of things they need to know and want to know at their age; and on the whole this is what they are doing if they're working on their own: they're able to come and ask the questions they require. . . . '

Mr Freeman was a little more cautious. 'It depends entirely on the nature of the topic. I'm quite sure about this: the more they *can* be made to do themselves the better. But even so one's got to be a bit careful.'

Mr Black spoke about the difficulties of independent activity, defined in terms of class project work.

'I think the danger here is that although you can get some very good work . . . it perhaps gives added time for the slackers to slack; and I also think that it puts an extra burden on the teacher – particularly in a school like this where you've got a good town library but hopeless from the point of individual activities. You are the one who gets the books. You are the one who runs up and down stairs because the pupil is living in the back of beyond and you find that on that particular morning the mobile library hasn't been able to get to them. I think there ought to be a balance – heaven knows what it actually is. I find with my own teaching the balance goes towards what you not very flatteringly call "passive receptivity".'

Independent activity of this nature is often centred on teaching material such as illustrations, documents and maps, and the teacher made it clear that these would be used where appropriate.

'Take, for example,' said Mr Freeman, 'a reproduction of part of the Domesday survey taught in the first year. This would be typed out on little strips of paper. The master taking the form would give them out and the boys might make an illustrated map of part of the area marking C–, F– and all the rest of them; and then in little rectangles on the map might record what's recorded in the chapter about that particular village. That's just one example.'

Mr Neville talked about using the Magna Carta.

'I think the thing to do with Magna Carta is to give it to the class – the class has a transcript – and then you actually pull it to pieces with the boys in so far as they're able to use it. This is in the first year. It's not all that easy. The language is not too bad; but it's a little difficult sometimes putting the study over in relation to the very different ideas of the time. But I do feel that boys have got to be able to read documents. I mean, if they can see a reproduction on the board, jolly good. But they also want to be able to actually *look* at it and they've got to get something out of it.'

Mr Black and Miss Denton stressed the displays of material they put up; and Miss Spender had this to say about the use her department makes of photographs and documents:

'Very often photographs and postcards are put up to ask questions; and then time is spent in class answering them. Documents we use quite a bit in the fifth and sixth forms – duplicated copies. About once a term we have people from the local record office who come with a collection of archives on a particular period. We have typewritten questionnaires and the children have to go round and look at them and answer questions.'

Mr Neville and Miss Spender talked about project work of a rather different nature.

'At C– people have just dug up a medieval sanctuary. Now, I'd like to take a class of boys out to C– for a day and let them actually scrape away the earth from some bones and then come back and do a month's work on medieval conditions related to this. . . . But making little cardboard cubes and putting them together to make a pyramid – no. . . . You've got to actually go out and *handle* history; and I don't think you can get very far by handling imitation history.'

Miss Spender spoke of field work she does with her more junior forms.

'We take them, for example, into the city and give them a series of questions and problems and things to find out, say about the construction of the walls . . . in other words, make them walk around and look and examine the walls and say why, for example, they are irregular at certain points.'

However, such field work is often difficult to organise. There are practical difficulties, as Miss Denton pointed out.

'Field work – visits – these have occasionally been done with groups or forms but this is very difficult and disrupts the school day and timetable. Therefore they are mainly done through the history society (membership third to fifth forms); and we find Saturday visits increasingly difficult. Girls over fifteen often have regular

Saturday work . . . and younger ones (unlike boys!) are often expected to help in the home. Only at the end of the Summer term is one school day allowed to be used for a History Society excursion.' Secondly, in the fourth and fifth years there is less time for independent activity because of the demands of the external examination; and at the five schools field and project work of all kinds features less prominently during the G C E years.

Yet whether field and project work or note taking and making are the methods used, each is a means of achieving certain goals or objectives; and the questionnaire tried to sum up the history teaching situation by asking the teachers what they hoped to achieve by the end of the fifth year.

Question 31 (see p. 136) asked them to rank in order a list of ten aims; but all felt uncomfortable at having to structure the sweeping generalisations they were given.

Miss Denton remarked appositely that 'you might as well ask someone to place the various vitamins in order of their importance to the human body': and Mr Freeman wrote: 'I find it impossible to do this one. I think it is impossible to place these aims in any significant order.' He went on to say: 'With regard to your last aim (to enable the children to pass the 'O' level examination) we pay little attention to this in the first four years and a very great deal in the fifth.'

It is more useful therefore to look at the points the teachers noted down for question 32 ('What do you hope to have achieved by the beginning of the fourth year . . . ?'). Mr Black listed the following aims:

1. To teach children to think and to doubt both the textbook and myself.
2. To sympathise and understand – different problems, different people, different attitudes.
3. To begin to put our own society into some kind of historical perspective.
4. To have banished some ignorance.

It seems clear that he is concerned with emotional as well as mental goals, and that he sees history learning as something which involves the whole personality. These aims are held by all the teachers, and phrases such as 'development of interest and enjoyment' (Miss Denton), 'taking notice of the history around them' (Mr Freeman) or 'an appreciation and understanding of other men's ideas and achievements' (Miss Spender) would be accepted by them all – partly perhaps because of their high level of generality.

The teachers gave a sharper idea of what they hoped their subject would mean for their pupils when they talked about specific teaching situations. For example, all used the word 'reality' when talking about the use they make in class of documentary evidence. Mr Neville makes this point:

'Documents can invoke a sense of reality. You can see this with children. It's almost as though they've received a blow – 'Look, it's real'. Then, secondly, with some people it goes a long way beyond this because they're not satisfied with this sense of reality. It will then stimulate them to ask questions; it will lead them to start thinking for themselves. It doesn't happen as often as we would like.'

Miss Denton echoed his attitude when she said: 'In so far as anyone has any kind of personal contact . . . it becomes more real to you.' Mr Freeman, discussing leet court records, mentioned one he used to give when he taught in the North – 'I remember one in particular referring to an 'unruly, unlawful sow' in twelfth-century Preston which I thought evoked a splendid impression of the medieval term' – and Mr Black referred to 'a sense of awe' which a reproduction of Charles I's death warrant could arouse.

The word 'reality' was used in a different context. Miss Spender had been talking about field work in the city and explained the purpose of the expedition to the walls.

'Town children I've noticed aren't very observant – don't use their eyes at all. Unless you really make them look at things they're not very much aware of what they are seeing. And again they enjoy doing this: this is, if you like, like the documents – real. This is evidence, proof to them that the city was an important port; that the French wanted to destroy it and that the city followed the king's orders and put the walls up. It's the activity of doing things for themselves and finding out answers.'

Such graphic examples illustrate the sort of responses the teachers are looking for – an informed and sympathetic awareness of place and time which is central to the study of history.

Do the 'O' level syllabuses and examinations encourage such aims? It should be emphasised here that syllabus and examinations must be considered together, as the latter presumably is shaped by the former, looking for the qualities and aims the syllabus is supposed to exemplify. Of the five teachers only Miss Spender (whose fourth and fifth year pupils study the new London World Affairs course) spoke up in favour of the examination and its aims. She considered that it tested 'partly the ability to be logical, partly the ability to use information. I don't think they're just concerned with amassing factual information – especially the later periods. The questions, *as yet*, haven't become stereotyped – the kind of thing one can make them learn for the exam.'

The other teachers were fairly explicit about its limited nature. 'The *examiners* believe they are not testing detailed knowledge. It's always struck me that this is exactly what they are testing', said Mr Black.

Miss Denton echoed this opinion; and Mr Neville said fairly bluntly:

'What it does not test is the ability to produce a reasoned argument based on historical material in the boy's possession which he hasn't put together on a previous occasion. 'O' level history, after all, isn't meant to do this. 'O' level history is meant to test whether a boy has the power to memorise a certain mass of material and to reproduce it in coherent form.'

Mr Freeman added to this by saying:

'It measures a certain amount of second degree knowledge – factual knowledge which boys have absorbed and in some cases have understood and in some cases have not understood. There's a lot of unintelligent recognition. It tests the learning of facts: methodicalness: the ability to select a number of relevant facts and arrange them in a reasonably intelligent plan. Does it test literacy? Examiners seem to take little notice. I've known illiterate boys get a "one". Bombarding the examiners with facts produces good results. It rests above all the ability to absorb facts; and that's why I'm so dissatisfied with it.'

In the opinion of four of the teachers therefore the 'O' level history examination is concerned principally with the display of fragments of knowledge and leaves largely untouched the comprehension and analysis, the responding and valuing which they hope to achieve through their teaching.

All five teachers try to prevent the 'O' level examination from dominating their fourth and fifth year syllabuses, and in spite of its restricting effect, continue to uphold the aims they value. It seems right therefore to conclude this section with three comments made at the end of the interviews, for these represent and emphasise the views of the teachers.

'I think history should produce the beginnings of social insight – a first introduction to an analytical look at one's fellows and the society in which we live. . . .' (Mr Freeman).

'One aim is to develop what I call a sense of judgment – the ability to see different points of view and different sides to any question. This I think is important; and one can probably do this through history, particularly where the thing isn't immediate and one doesn't come with prejudices already' (Miss Spender).

Finally from Mr Black.

'Through history I think you probably are "initiated" into all kinds of things. . . . You are showing them that there's more in life than the latest top ten or boy friend or hair style. This is something you're offering.'

These are the sort of experiences that the broad, catholic character of history can offer, experience into which the senior history teachers hope to initiate their pupils. What then are the reactions of the pupils to the teachers' classroom practice?

THE PUPILS SPEAK

Presentation is the crux of the matter for the pupils. The following section explores this statement and shows that what really concerns them is the particular classroom situation and the teaching carried on week by week; and the pupils tend to evaluate the subject in terms of the teacher's handling of the class and the teaching techniques used, rather than through an objective consideration of the importance or relevance of the material.

The pupils were asked whether they enjoyed the history they learned in their first three years at grammar school more than the 'O' level course they had just started. Nearly half answered in the affirmative. Now of course there is a tendency to look back nostalgically to first and second years; and the rebelliousness of adolescence may in any case have made some express discontent with their present lot. What reasons, then, did the pupils give for this preference for pre 'O' level history?

' . . . it was more varied and we did projects', wrote a girl from Benborough.

'History now just becomes one long period of notes but before topics were very different from each other and far less boring' (F G S).

' . . . there was a wider variety of subject and more interesting' (N G S).

'I found the history in my first three years at grammar school was more varied. The work we are doing now is all the same period of history and it becomes monotonous. Also in the first three years we used to do projects etc. and this made work more interesting' (S G S).

Three boys from Benborough made implicit or explicit reference to the pressures of 'O' level.

'1st year history deals with primitive England and there are far less dates and complicated facts to remember. History gets more disagreeable as it progresses.'

"I enjoyed the history learned in the first three years better because there was no feeling that all the work was done only in aid of passing the G C E 'O' level.'

'In the first three years the work was not so concentrated and there were less dates and facts crammed in. The periods themselves were more enjoyable as the teacher had more time to explain things well and relate them to other periods in history and other topics going on at the same time in history'.

Few revealing explanations came from those who answered 'Indifferent' or 'No' to the question on pre 'O' level history. A Fairport boy sharply pointed out the bluntness of the question. 'There is not really an answer to this. The facts about all history have to be learned. There are too many facts.' A pupil from Neil noted: 'It was much the same except for the speed at which it was covered,' and a Benborough boy wrote: 'I am being taught history in the same way that I was taught before the 'O' level course, so I like it just as well'. A boy from Fairport made a particularly telling remark: 'During this period praise was given for neat maps and diagrams rather than any actual historical knowledge.'

At N G s one boy criticised the superficial coverage of history in the first three years, while another commented on the relevance of the 'O' level syllabus. Such remarks were infrequent. It seemed that many of the pupils do feel that 'O' level history is rushed and overcrowded with fragments of knowledge, and that the syllabuses give them little time to think round the material.

The answers to question 13 of the pupils' questionnaire, which asked for more specific information about teaching techniques, give emphasis to this conclusion. Here the pupils were asked to assess activities they might have pursued in history in their first three years at grammar school and by ticks to indicate on five point scales their interest in the activities and whether they found them helpful in learning the history, and on a four point scale the frequency with which they pursued them. The full question and the table are given on pp. 138-9.[1]

Now it must be admitted that the question is open to criticism. In the first place, it is doubtful whether the pupils were really recording their attitude towards history in the first three years, and it would seem that their answers give a more accurate picture of history as it is taught in the fourth year. This assumption is based mainly on classroom observation made in October and November 1965, a limited appraisal which seemed to receive confirmation from the pupils' responses to question 13. Secondly, the different activities listed in the table are not clearly delineated and the pupils' interpretations may differ. There are not only the difficulties here of differences between the child's eye view and the teacher's but between the children of one school. For example, when is class discussion taking place? When the teacher is asking questions? When there is a regular shindy? What is the distinction between historical documents, reproductions of pictures and photographs of historical material? What is a written project? Thirdly, the rubric at the top is complicated and some pupils failed to follow the instructions exactly, recording their interest in and the usefulness of activities which they said they had 'never' pursued. (In these cases the first two entries were ignored for the purposes of the analysis.) Telling though these criticisms are, it is felt that the picture which emerges is a useful one and justifies the setting of the question. In conjunction with the interviews a full account of the history classroom situation can be built up.

An analysis of the answers to question 13 shows that most pupils consider history lessons to consist of learning facts, reading textbooks, listening to the class teacher, note making and taking dictated notes. The great majority of pupils indicated that these five activities are pursued at least once a week. No other activity on the list has anything like such a

---

[1] When analysing the pupils' answers to this question, the activities were taken separately, and the number of ticks in each column for the five schools expressed as a percentage of the total sample: for example, 0·8 per cent of the pupils find 'learning facts' 'very enjoyable', 8·4 per cent 'enjoyable' – and so on. These percentages were then drawn in histogram form. For each of the twenty listed activities, therefore, three histograms ('interest', 'use', 'frequency') were drawn, to give visual representation of the pupils' answers. The histograms are shown in Appendix V, p. 149.

high percentage ticking the '1 + per week' column.[1] The implication of this for history teaching is important. The pupils have shown that history only too often seems to be a case of learning fragments of information – 'facts' – which never become appropriated because the mind has not worked round them. Learning has never gone beyond the stage of memorisation. A number of pupils referred indirectly to this in the interviews when talking about 'O' level examinations and the research history tests.

MB: 'Would you prefer to take examinations similar to the research history tests for 'O' level?

1ST GIRL (B G S): Yes, definitely.

2ND GIRL: No, I don't think so. In an 'O' level paper you've got a certain period to do, haven't you? and you learn all of that and you can expand all your knowledge on a certain question.

1ST GIRL: I think this sort of paper would be easier because you don't have to write in such detail; and it's very hard to learn the facts off by heart. You learn the facts but they don't seem relative to us . . .'

A boy from Benborough contrasted the application of knowledge which the research tests required with the approach needed for 'O' level papers: 'I prefer these (the research tests). I think applying knowledge in the way these have done is better than just reeling it off. You tend to remember it better if you apply it.' And many pupils mentioned the rote learning which 'O' level seems to demand. ' . . . with the questions that we're likely to get asked we've learned the answers by heart and we've gone over and over them in class. We've learned them almost parrot fashion from a book and we can just recite them' (D G S); ' . . . the sort of stuff you can do for 'O' level you can learn parrot like' (F G S).

A boy from N G S (in reply to the question 'would you like to do similar tests for "O" level?') said 'Yes, I think so; but it's not much a test of knowledge is it? I mean it wouldn't do as a substitute for examinations.'

MB: What do the examinations test?

BOY: What you've learned over the past year in history.

MB: But does it really test whether you understand it or not?

BOY: No, it just tests whether you know it.

[1] The table below shows the number of ticks for all schools expressed as percentages of the total number for the '1 + per week' column of these five activities.

Activity	Ticks in '1 + per week column', as percentage of total number of pupils.
1. Learning facts	50·8
3. Reading text books	74·8
4. Listening	91·0
5. Making own notes	63·4
6. Taking dictated notes	84·8

'Learning generalisations' has a percentage of 29·2 for the '1 + per week' column, 'formal essays', 25·4. The only other activity with a percentage of greater than 10 for this column is 'drawing maps and diagrams' (12·8 per cent).

A Scarcombe girl said she would prefer examinations similar to the research tests for 'O' level.

MB: Because it's easier?

GIRL: No, not just because it's easier but because it seems to have a completely different idea. . . . You didn't have to know the historical facts. You had to be able to apply them to something else.

The pupils' view of history as a subject which involves memorisation but little application of knowledge was mentioned in a different context. I had been asking about project work.

MB: 'Do you do many this year?

GIRL (s G s): We haven't this year in history: we have in geography.

MB: Do you like geography?

GIRL: Yes – but when you've got history to follow there's so much to learn.

MB: More to learn than, say, in maths?

GIRL: Yes. In maths, you've got to learn the method and then use it for the exam paper.

To the pupils the facts which dominate history are dates, unconnected groups of figures as difficult and disagreeable as telephone numbers to remember.[1] But it is facts of this order which will be tested in the examination, and the effort must be made to commit the information to memory. As one boy put it, when asked if he thought there was too much note learning in history: 'Well, there is I think: but then how else can you do it? There isn't much else except learning facts and dates and things, it seems at the moment. I mean, nobody's made any new type of history . . . I mean, the only way you can learn about past things is to learn it all off parrot fashion.'

How is the information put across? Over ninety per cent of the pupils indicated that listening to the class teacher is something they do at least once a week. The teachers made it clear that the spoken word is their main classroom method – that the children must be told. The crucial point is the manner and purpose of the telling. Does it involve and illuminate the understanding? Or does it merely deaden so that the words slide over the pupils? The impression given in the interviews was that too often the pupils feel that they are being talked 'at' rather than 'with'; and the answers to the activity 'discussion' (listed in question 13) seem to lend weight to this view. Over thirty per cent of the pupils were prepared to say they 'never' have discussion, and thirty-five per cent that it happens only once a term or so. In spite of the semantic difficulties, the implication is clear. For most of the time the pupils do not feel involved or committed. The history taught does not affect them because they are not being made to grapple with it. The point came up constantly in the interviews.

[1] In the questionnaire the pupils were asked to name the kind of historical facts they found hard to remember. The approximate percentages in each school who put down 'dates' are as follows: Benborough, 75; Daymer, 88; Fairport, 55; Neil, 62; Scarcombe, 78. Of the total number of pupils 44·2 per cent 'Dislike', 17·4 per cent 'Strongly dislike' learning facts. 17·0 per cent find them 'very helpful', 49·6 per cent 'helpful' in learning history.

'The teacher just tells us about it; and then we write it up or take notes and it doesn't really stay. I think if you took more part in learning about it instead of merely telling us and then making us write it up, it would be better. I mean, if we discussed it together' (D G S).

'I think the way the teacher stands up in front and just tells you everything and writes them down on the blackboard and you copy them down should be changed. I think it should be more co-operation between the two, discussion and things like that' (D G S).

'I think that it could be made more interesting by involving the class more, rather than just taking notes and telling you "this is what happened". I think you can involve the class in class discussion' (F G S).

'If it's a project you do more your own work. If you do it like we're doing at the moment, China, the teacher just *tells* you and writes on the board, doesn't she?' (S G S).

To involve a class – to establish what Martin Buber called the 'I thou' relationship – is no easy matter. There are disciplinary difficulties, as a boy pointed out when asked why he thought there was so little discussion: 'There's usually an outcry and people get a bit wild.' Or sometimes in a girls' school there are the problems of breaking down a barrier of silence: 'We tried it once but only three of us were talking plus the teacher.'

Once these practical difficulties are overcome, there is the much more complex problem of how to draw from a class the information which can lead to understanding. Such subtle questioning, which is never cross examining, still less a loose chat, compels the pupils to re-examine old assumptions and face new problems. It puts them, perhaps, in the position of the research worker who makes deductions from the material he has assembled by asking himself the right questions. The drawback, of course, is that progress *seems* to be slower. There is less opportunity for the teacher to skim through the years, dispensing facts and dates with a liberality which overpowers the pupils. Yet the syllabus has to be covered. A number of pupils remarked on this when they were explaining why they had so little discussion.

'There isn't enough time' (girl, B G S).

'We don't get the opportunity' (boy, B G S).

'The sort of teaching we have at the moment explains why we have no discussions. The master does most of the talking and therefore he gets right down to the important things. He doesn't deal with trivial matters' (F G S).

'I like having discussions but we don't often have them. I don't really think we have enough time to get through the work and spend a long time on discussing' (D G S).

Listening to the teacher is not unpleasant. It is, after all, not very hard work. Note taking and making is less popular, partly because of the effort it demands, partly because it is done so frequently. In spite of what the senior history teachers said, dictated notes, or notes copied from the blackboard, seem to be a very frequent activity, pursued more often, according to the pupils, than individually made notes. Surprisingly, the former are enjoyed more than the latter. There are two factors which help to explain this. First, taking dictated or copied notes requires little effort; secondly, pupils feel more secure with notes given them by the teacher.

'I don't mind taking dictated notes – I don't like taking my own. I never know what to put in or what to leave out. When you're taking notes from a book you don't know which are the important parts' (D G S).

'I'm always afraid you're going to leave something out when taking notes from a book' (girl, B G S).

The interviews, however, showed that the pupils are less favourably disposed to note taking than their questionnaire answers indicated. The fairly large section who said they were 'indifferent' to note taking and making turned into a more outspoken body. Practically every pupil had the same answer when asked what activities in history class he or she disliked.

GIRL (B G S): 'I don't like taking notes. I don't mind taking them when people are talking but having to make notes from the book and reading through and making notes.

MB: Do you know what to put down?

GIRL: Well, you generally end up by just changing round the sentences in the book and copying down what was in the book.'

'I hate just having to take down notes' (D G S).

'When you're just being chicken fed. Where you take it out of a book and copy it down into a notebook and then just learn the dates' (F G S).

'Taking notes' (N G s).

'I don't like writing notes' (S G s).

Is this perhaps just the natural laziness of the pupils revealing itself? In the interviews many of them gave rational explanations of their dislike. Those, for example, who condemned dictated notes spoke of the lack of thought they encouraged.

'The thing is when you're dictating you tend to write it down and not take it in. But when you discuss it first you get the idea of what it's about and you understand it: then you write it down in your own words' (girl B G S).

'Unless you concentrate hard it's just like a writing exercise, quite honestly. It's quite a temptation to let your mind go blank and then carry on writing' (F G S).

Others made it clear that it was the monotony of a diet of note taking unrelieved by other nourishment that made them dislike it so much.

Only in Scarcombe grammar school was there any spoken indication that note taking was enjoyable.

'I like taking notes; most people don't. I do. Most of the time you've got to, the teacher tells you all about it. You listen, then she puts notes up and you've got to enlarge upon it. If you've got to do that it helps you to remember.'

But this was one remark in an expanse of criticism, a dreary desert where as far as the eye could see row upon row of school children sit, writing endless notes. But what can be done?

'I don't think you can really change it. You've got to get the people to learn the dates – you've got to get them to take notes and that . . .' (F G S).

'You've got to have it because we're in a hurry . . .' (F G S).

'You've got to have it because the master thinks it's the easiest way of doing it – getting through the syllabus. . . .' (F G S).

It is largely a matter of convenience and simplicity which prompts the teacher to rely on note taking. The examination demands a high proportion of memorised information. This is something the pupils must be told; and the spoken word must be condensed into note form so that the facts can easily be committed to memory. The textbook, too, will be relied on heavily, as the pupils made clear in their answers to question 13. Here is another source of predigested history, laden with dates, which the children can dehydrate into note form. It makes a convenient homework or an easy lesson – though as one or two pupils indicated, the textbook rarely succeeds in illuminating the understanding.

GIRL (S G S): 'I dislike reading: being left on our own just to get on with it.
MB: Does this happen often?
GIRL: Well, for homework we get reading and I find it difficult to settle down . . .
MB: With the old telly blaring in the background?
GIRL: Yes, that's right. I'd rather write an essay – find something out for myself than read it and be expected to remember it all for the next lesson.'

Two pupils talked about reading in class.

'I don't like reading . . . I mean, if we read in class there seems to be so many people around me that I just can't take it in' (S G S).

'I think it's when he tells us to read the book,' replied a boy from Fairport when asked about the activities he disliked. 'You read it once; then he spends rather a long time doing something else while you finish; he starts talking to someone and you spend rather a long time doing nothing.'

Once a month or so, as an alternative to note taking and textbook reading, the pupils write a formal essay, disliked by both children and teachers. For the former it means a hard evening's work to accumulate the necessary factual information; for the latter anything up to two hours' marking. But practice in writing the thirty or forty minute examination essay has to be given in the fourth and fifth years, and the formal essay can give a good indication of the amount of material the pupils have memorised.

Little time seems to be left for other activities. Date and time charts are made occasionally, maps and diagrams more frequently. Such activities are popular with some. A B G S boy, for example, wrote explaining his liking for the Indian mutiny: 'because it makes a change from British history and there are complicated maps involved in it. N B – I like drawing maps.'

But for others it often seems a case of copying trivialities from the board or book.

> 'I think at the moment there's rather a lot of time spent on – shall we say – the Bessemer thing: we had a whole diagram on that today. I fail to see the use of that. I forget how the Bessemer process worked. All I want to know is the effect it had on industry which he dismissed in a couple of lines.'

The other listed activities are pursued only very occasionally, and it is clear that the pupils consider them peripheral. Examining documents, pictures or photographs seems to have little connection with the ordinary grind of history; though perhaps greater understanding of, say, the first empire could be achieved in a lesson based on David's 'Coronation of Napoleon' than with forty minutes of notes. Local history, too, seems to play little part according to the pupils' responses; but an afternoon spent at the local records office looking at reports of a commission on the town workhouse (a building which is now part of the hospital and just across the road from the school) might interest the children in the question of nineteenth-century poor law administration more than a period or two of chalk and talk on the Poor Law Amendment Act. Films and filmstrips are rarely seen. One girl spoke for many of the pupils when she said:

> 'I'd have less people telling you things and more films showing you: people telling you things and them happening at the same time. We had a film on the period after the First World War; and it was much more interesting than being told that Lloyd George said "A land fit for heroes" and all that. It's much more interesting if you see this chap standing up and making a great song and dance about it, and then seeing how nothing really happened.'

A boy referred to the successful use of pictures in his first year at grammar school.

> ' . . . the first year I came to school we had I thought the best master for history. He used to have pictures – not much writing done – more getting the facts to you in your head rather than on paper to be learned later . . . '

The pupils indicated that debates and talks given by the children are also infrequent. Many teachers would question the usefulness of these activities in history. Psychologically, however, simply standing in front of a class can be salutary, and the pupils themselves (though none will confess to enjoying the experience) often take immense pains in preparing their talks. If carefully handled, the short talk can provide a means of pooling information (for example, in group project work) and be a useful introduction to a period of general discussion.

Project work, however, demands a careful analysis, partly because the children had much to say about it, partly because the teachers were all convinced that 'independent activity' was something which should be encouraged. Yet nearly thirty per cent of the pupils indicated that they 'never' did projects and over sixty per cent that they were given project work only once a term. There is of course the difficulty of definition here. What exactly is 'project work'? The pupils were fairly clear that it means an assignment of work which they do largely on their own, or in a group, with help and direction from the teacher. The nature of the project work will have been carefully mapped out beforehand by the teacher and the sources of information indicated. It might be work on documents and photographs, or it could be field work where the pupils have to investigate a town, battle site, building, museum or what ever. More usually, however, the project will be one where most of the information is obtained (sometimes rather haphazardly) from secondary sources. But whatever form the project takes, the crucial part is the planning the teacher puts in beforehand. The pupils must be clear what they are looking for, where they can find information and how they are to present it. Otherwise the activity degenerates into an aimless bustle and becomes merely a 'concession to restlessness'.

The pupils were outspoken in their approval of project work. 'I like that. That makes learning easy. You've got to do the looking up and everything yourself and something's bound to sink in, rather than if you're just taking it down in dictation' (girl B G S).

'If it's a project you do more your own work' (S G S).

Here the personal nature of the activity is emphasised: the work is made your own; and a boy carried this a stage further by talking about the independence gained. 'You could work your own hours when you like. You're more prepared to do it and turn in good work' (B G S).

Others talked about the pleasures of discovery; the feeling of satisfaction when the explanation is come across unaided.

'We could discover things for ourselves and not just have them told' (D G S).

'I like private research – then writing your own notes on it' (F G S).

'I enjoyed spending time on the French revolution and Napoleon because we had to search for information ourselves and not just make dictated notes' (N G S).

'I like to do projects myself – discover things for myself' (S G S).

A boy spoke about studying a topic 'in depth' through project work.

'Well, we did one where we had to do an essay on Waterloo over the holiday. . . . I got engrossed in that. And I think if I go into something in depth I enjoy anything. But I have to go really into it' (F G S).

What is implied here by the phrase 'in depth'? Not merely the accumulation of more information about the topic. The pupil in some way has been able to feel the reality of the period. This was the tenor of a girl's response to the questionnaire item which asked: 'Do you enjoy spending time on one topic in history, covering it in detail and studying it in depth?' She wrote: 'This enables you to understand it better and perhaps imagine it actually happening' (S G S). Two boys from Neil wrote in the same vein. 'I like to know the details behind a certain topic because I feel it makes it more real'; 'I find that I understand it more and I try to imagine myself there at that time.'

These are the sort of insights that carefully planned project work can provide.

There are of course two factors which make the organisation of project work difficult. First, none of the five schools has a fully equipped history room, and the teachers emphasised the difficulties they could experience in getting necessary basic equipment such as cupboards or display boards, while the science or language departments seem to have no trouble in obtaining large grants of money. Secondly, and more important, project work is not usually geared to the 'O' level syllabus which demands wide coverage. One boy remarked: 'The trouble with projects is that you don't get much done', meaning that coverage in the chronological sense is often small.

These factors are not insuperable; nor are the problems of organisation. Project work however is not an easy way of ensuring successful history lessons. Careful planning, it has been stressed, is an essential prerequisite for worthwhile independent activity; during classwork periods the pupils will need much guidance; the finished work must be assessed carefully by the teacher and discussed in class afterwards. In one of the interviews a boy commented with some bitterness on an inadequately marked project he had done the previous year. 'Well, it's just pointless if that's the thing that's going to happen, isn't it sir? You tend to write a lot of irrevelant detail down. . . . You won't bother to revise it because it'll be so boring.' Project work can become as irrelevant and pointless as dictated notes. When well organised it can be engrossing and illuminating, an educational activity which really does contribute to personal fulfilment.

Personal fulfilment is hardly a phrase the pupils would use when talking about the purpose of classroom activity; and in order to gain some impression of the contributions they consider the teaching of history can make to their intellectual and emotional outlook the final items of the questionnaire asked for the pupils' reaction to the history they had learned so far. Such an approach is perhaps unduly blunt and once again the way was laid open for clichés which had little to do with the pupil's real attitude. In any case what a pupil believes his gains to have been may differ radically from the sort of understandings he has actually acquired. The chance remarks of the interviews and, in particular, the written answers to the research tests were more helpful in building up a picture of what the pupils had gained from their study of history.

However, the questionnaire answers make a starting point. They certainly show that the majority of the pupils are prepared to acknowledge history as an important subject – a recognition perhaps that some under-standing of time, people and place is necessary for man to reach maturity. Many however thought of history in meliorist terms, showing a slightly smug and complacent attitude. The following comments are typical.

'I would definitely say that I have gained a more lasting picture of the way in which people of the world have progressed, as in the study of remote civilisations and such modern topics as the industrial and agricultural revolutions. In addition my study of history has stimulated my interest to learn more history which will probably be more complicated (boy, B G S).

'I have got a general idea of how the commonwealth was founded and of how England became a highly industrialised country' (F G S).

'Yes, definitely. I have gained (and am gaining) an idea of the foundation of our system and customs in this country' (N G S).

'Most history, whether a long period or not, proves this, that things are improving all the time' (girl, B G S).

The research history tests gave additional information here. The pupils were asked in one question (number 8, paper I) to write about the changes that would have taken place over a seven hundred year period (1066 to 1750); nearly all noted changes for the better. I asked some of them about this in the interviews: did they, by and large, see history as the story of things getting better and better? and most agreed without hesitation that this was the way they saw it. One or two qualified their answers. 'Except weapons' (N G S); 'apart from the cost of living and prices going up' (F G S).

Two boys from Benborough were a little more cautious.

1ST BOY: In some respects. Civilisation generally improves. But on the other hand as population increases so the poverty increases.

2ND BOY: I think if you look at it logically as technology and science advances the conditions of the people should get better provided you don't have tyrants like Hitler.

MB: Can you think of anything that's changed for the worse in 1960?

2ND BOY: The position of the people in Africa.

1ST BOY: China was once a great empire and the conditions have gone down.

2ND BOY: I think in 1066 if you had a man who was determined to rule the land, well, he could only do so much. Whereas nowadays you get a couple of bombers and a few tanks and he can go practically anywhere.

It is perhaps hardly surprising that many children of the space age should see history as a prelude to the 1960s, an attitude which contains much of the flamboyant optimism Macaulay displayed when writing of the constitutional achievements of the nineteenth century. Pride in our scientific and technological advances is natural; yet I believe that we fail in our task as history teachers if our lessons are designed to inculcate only this attitude. Relevance, it has been argued, need not mean subordination of the past to the twentieth century; history can exist in its own right for children, can evoke a credibility which evokes humility and a proper sense of evolutionary growth. This understanding of the organic nature of man's past is very different from the crude meliorist attitude; it sobers rather than exalts; it cherishes the past rather than destroys; it shows that we, too, have far to travel. Such maturity of outlook can be detected in two comments from girls at Daymer grammar school:

'I think I have more a sense of proportion because I didn't use to think that the Tudors and Stuarts were very far apart but now I realise that they are as far apart from each other as we are from the Stuarts';

'I think I have gained a sense of realising the length of time which has elapsed and the part we are living in is very short in comparison . . .'

and in some of the interviews, when, for example, the pupils were talking about project work they had done, it was possible to sense the exhilaration, the feeling of release and freedom of mental movement, such study for its own sake gave them – an experience which can be the prelude to a deeper insight.

Other pupils wrote about the understandings they had achieved in somewhat conventional and stilted language:

'I think I am getting a clearer picture of how people lived, worked and what they believed in . . . ' (D G S).

'One can see the future in our history and if we are careful by seeing our fate we can avoid wars etc. So many people have given their all for us that we may live in peace. I think it is right that we should know and honour what they did for us' (F G S).

'I think I have gained a sense of change in this country, politically, socially, churchwise and conditions of education' (N G S).

The girls of Scarcombe made specific and frequent reference to the world affairs syllabus, and comments such as these again affirmed their liking for the course.

'It is easier to understand world affairs and the work of a government today.'

'I think modern history has made one more aware of the problems of the world.'

'I have a sense of understanding of situations in the world today.'

'I think that my study of these sort of subjects is very helpful in a better understanding of world affairs.'

For many, however, school history holds no promise of such initiation.

The weekly pattern of lessons deadens with 'the same routine: you listen read and write'. Such lack of stimulation produces apathy as often as not. The strong antipathy felt by the following two boys was seldom shown in the questionnaires or interviews. Both pupils want to study science subjects in the sixth form.

1ST BOY: 'Who wants to know the Chartists failed anyway? . . . Surely you should look to the future not the past.

2ND BOY: Physics I find helps you with the present as well as for the future. But history outside school – well, I don't find any use at all.

1ST BOY: I think science is the thing that is needed now. I like chemistry. I want to be a chemist. I don't see any importance in history.

MB: Can you imagine a world in which all history had been abolished?

1ST BOY (*laughing*): It'd be great!

MB: What would the consequences be? More happy school children?

1ST BOY: I suppose you must learn history to some extent. But only as generalisations – nothing exact.

MB: You – a scientist – saying this?

1ST BOY: Only for history.

MB: It's good enough for history?'

He seemed to think modern history would be more relevant.

1ST BOY: 'I think we should have modern history after the second world war – much more important.

2ND BOY: More relevant to us today.'

But the first boy's dislike of history soon swamped this idea, and he spoke with bitterness:

1ST BOY: 'We don't object to the historians sticking to history: but why make us learn history? That's what I think.

MB: I think you've got the idea that history is all learning up facts and dates.

2ND BOY: Well, that's the way it affects us at the moment.'

The point that emerges from this diatribe against history is the faint recognition of the subject's importance, a tacit acceptance that it is, after all, part of one's identity. But it would seem that the way in which the boys have been taught has produced this reaction to school history, and it may well be that once they move up into the sixth form they will make a point of avoiding any further contact with the subject.

CONCLUSIONS AND RECOMMENDATIONS

It is perhaps not surprising that much of the pupils' evidence is of a predictable nature: they have answered in ways that most history teachers would expect. More than this, part of what the children wrote and said would apply equally to other subjects – lecture and note taking, for example, can form the staple fare of pupils learning English or geography. But some of their comments echo the doubts which the history teachers expressed; and though the pupils' evidence perhaps is of a commonplace nature and suffers from the outspokenness of youth, this two-sided picture gives added force to the arguments in favour of changing our classroom practice.

For change is badly needed. If these pupils are to be believed, history lessons are often dull and seldom make demands; and the picture they present could and probably does apply to the majority of secondary schools. The lecturing, note taking and note making which seem to be such frequent occurences rarely challenge the pupils or illuminate their understanding. Such challenge and illumination, which are 'means to clarification of the self and of the world', can only occur when there is involvement which creates tensions and leads to mental activity. Involvement therefore is the essential prerequisite for purposeful learning.

But it is involvement which is lacking in most history lessons. The lack may be caused partly by the demands of the 'O' level history examination which appears to most history teachers and pupils to put a premium on the retention of information and to have almost no regard for historical understanding and the exploration of ideas; and evidence from this enquiry shows that teaching in the fourth and fifth years is restricted by this view of the examination. It is also partly a result of limited facilities, for it is difficult to introduce more varied teaching when the desks, display boards and storage space are inadequate and there is no blackout for the windows. The lesson tends almost inevitably to consist of exposition and note taking, as these are the quickest and easiest means of giving the pupils the information required for the examination. But as the pupils (and certain of the teachers) pointed out, films and filmstrips can often present the same information in more attractive and dynamic fashion; and this can be the prelude to a critical, historical consideration of issues and problems which the more passive tasks of listening or note taking seldom engender. Documents and photographs, too, if carefully chosen, can also provide a more vivid commentary than chalk, talk and notes. We are therefore confronted with a situation where both teachers and pupils are generally agreed on the superiority of certain types of approach, yet find themselves permanently at a disadvantage.

The problem however is more fundamental than this, and it is the whole concept of authoritarian teaching which the pupils question and find inadequate. Both the layout of the classrooms and the teaching which is carried on in them are legacies from the days when masters and mistresses instructed by question and answer, and pupils were drilled and disciplined into accepting without question the attitudes of their elders who always knew better. Adolescent children no longer accept this approach so readily; and more varied teaching is required if their interest is to be maintained, their imaginations stirred and their intellectual abilities and skills exercised. Such aims should shape all valid test procedures; and this is the particular concern of current work on examinations which is designed to stimulate and reflect the best classroom practice. Many history teachers, however, feel that success at 'O' level is often associated with the old authoritarian tradition, even though the examiners for years have complained in their published comments about rote learning and meaningless repetition of notes. There may be a tendency therefore for us to justify all our shortcomings by blaming an outside agency; we have, after all, the opportunity today with C S E and certain G C E boards to organise and assess our fourth and fifth year syllabuses internally under a mode 3 scheme.

Reorganisation under mode 3 is not of itself going to change our teaching techniques; but it might allow a closer connection between aims, classroom practice and assessment. This in its turn could lead to the rejection of teaching through instruction which seems to be the hall mark of many history lessons. The majority of pupils who took part in this enquiry seemed to think that in class they are talked 'at' rather than 'with'. The teacher 'just tells us about it . . . it doesn't really stay. I think it could be made more interesting by involving the class more, rather than just taking notes and telling you "this is what happened". I think you can involve the class in class discussion.'

The elements of confrontation and challenge seem to be missing. History is something about which the teacher tells the pupils, but which rarely involves their full interest. Here it would seem that the *introduction* of a theme is of crucial importance. As this and the previous chapter stress, practically any topic can be made relevant to children provided it is presented in the right manner. From the start the pupils must feel convinced that the subject matter is so worth while as to ensure their whole attention. In individual and group work a personal interest will be the starting point. For example, the boy mentioned in chapter 2 was attracted to the topic on Rhodes because his mother had lived in South Africa; the girl who had heard talk about the Second World War and had seen a film on Hitler's Germany had had her interest aroused in the problems of the rise and fall of the Nazi party. Often, however, the teacher has the task of introducing a theme to the whole class. The procedure in these cases must be determined not only by the interests, abilities and aptitudes of the pupils and the teacher but also by the nature of the subject matter. It could be that a local event or situation will provide an introduction. 'What does the class think about the action of the council in forbidding the gypsy encampment?' This leads to a discussion of the rights of gypsies, the question of public welfare and the welfare state. Perhaps a national issue will be used, for example the problems of raising the school leaving age. This gives relevance to a consideration of child labour, Factory Acts and the provision of education by local authorities. Whatever the starting point the intention is the same: to avoid the flat presentation of facts which will seem to have connection only with the examination syllabus. Instead the aim is to stimulate interest, to involve the pupils and to show the relevance of the material. History will then no longer be a dry catalogue of facts but a living vital subject in which fact and thought interact.

Once this basic interest has been secured, the possibilities are endless.

For example, there will be many opportunities for interrelation with other subjects. School syllabuses tend to concentrate on constitutional, political and diplomatic history. Full historical understanding, however, must be concerned with all facets of a period; and geography, sociology, literature, art, architecture, music, to name but a few, have vital contributions to make. Such contributions must not be extras tagged on as an unwilling concession to modern theories on the integration of subjects; they must form an essential part of the teaching. Here the arguments in favour of team teaching are particularly cogent. This can immeasurably strengthen the scope and variety of the syllabus and at the same time weaken the barriers between the humanities. The outline textbook, too, will no longer be adequate, and teachers will build up stocks of books, collections of documents and visual material of all kinds on a range of topics so that the variety of teaching can be matched by the material for class and homework.

A history department that is well equipped with books and other material will find the organisation of individual research and group schemes an easier matter; and pupils who have been introduced to a theme in the manner indicated will be prepared to embark on a project with enthusiasm and purpose. The pupils in this enquiry made it clear that well organised activity of this nature is intellectually rewarding – something that 'makes learning easy'; and the teachers too, though feeling themselves restricted by many factors, believe that 'the more they can be made to do themselves the better'.[1] A plea for more project work is not new, nor peculiar to history; but it is specially relevant to a subject which has been resistant to changes in teaching techniques. We tend to perpetuate in our lessons the methods by which history was taught fifty years ago, and we often forget that the historian's task can be as practical as the geographer's. Of course we are faced with the problem of collecting sufficient and suitable material, of course we are restricted by the limitations of our classrooms; but these difficulties are not insuperable, as many competent teachers have shown. History can be made a subject in which project work has an important place, where exploration and discovery take over from listening and writing.

This is not to suggest that projects are the panacea for all our teaching difficulties; it should be clear from what has already been written that exposition, questioning and discussion have a part to play, particularly when introducing and concluding a theme. Indeed, it is often the weaker teacher who tries to avoid the challenge and intellectual difficulties of the orthodox lesson by organising nothing but independent activity. What is needed is a balance: some exposition, some discussion, some project work. The argument can best be illustrated by giving four examples of the

[1] The Schools Council Examination Bulletin No. 18, *The Certificate of Secondary Education: the place of the Personal Topic – History* (H.M.S.O. London, 1968) stresses the popularity amongst both teachers and pupils of work of this nature. The Bulletin reports the results of an investigation into the running of Personal Topic work in C S E.

way in which work could be organised in the lower and middle school for pupils of average ability. For each of the first three years and for the fourth and fifth years, twelve lessons are taken, and methods and activities described which tie in with the syllabus discussed in the previous chapter. The lessons have been chosen to illustrate as many different learning situations as possible; and it has been assumed (perhaps rather unfairly – for few history teachers have all these advantages) that field work can be arranged, that projectors are available and that the department is well stocked with a varied assortment of history books and other material readily available for classroom use. Where methods are repeated (as for example with classroom project work through assignment cards) it has not been felt necessary to give details every time. The schemes make no mention of team teaching, either within the department or between departments, for the organisation of this is a highly individual matter and dependent on the particular school situation. Finally, it must be stressed that the suggested lessons are a personal choice and in no way pretend to be the ideal solution.

First year

Two forty-minute lessons a week
Term one: 12 lessons

THE FERTILE CRESCENT

Lesson 1: Exposition, questioning, discussion
General settling in period. Allocation of places for year's work. What do we mean by the word 'history'? Pupils give examples of famous characters from the past. Teacher builds up a time sequence on the board. When does history begin? What do we have before recorded history? Discovery of fire, agriculture, domestication of animals.

Lesson 2: Exposition, questioning, discussion
Meaning of the word 'archaeologist'. Importance of archaeologists in helping us to understand early civilisations. What do we mean by the word 'civilisation'? Issue of cyclostyled copies of year's syllabus. Introduce idea of 'world history'. Pupils turn to relevant page in history atlases and look at and discuss the features of the Fertile Crescent and Nile Valley. Teacher emphasises the importance of geography in the study of history.

Lesson 3: Discussion: mapwork
Outline map of Fertile Crescent and Egypt on the board, with a list of relevant name places to the side. Brief recap. of last lesson. Pupils turn to relevant page in history atlases and draw map of Middle East, looking up and marking down names noted on board. Board map will show correct area to be drawn.

Lesson 4: Introduction to project work on the Fertile Crescent
Explanation of the project: division of the class into three groups: issue of assignment cards. Three groups of ten each to be chosen, one to deal with the Sumerians, one with Babylonia and the Assyrians and one with the Hebrews. The task of each group is to produce a large display of illustrations, maps and short articles on their particular topic. For each group, assignment cards will show subtopics to be investigated, and suggestions of where the information can be found. Subtopics will be assigned to the pupils by the group leader. An example of an assignment card issued to each pupil in the 'Sumerian group' is given below.

The Sumerians
1. Who were the early settlers? Describe the country in which they settled. What is its modern name? How have people today found out about the Sumerians?
2. Read the story of the Flood in the Bible (Genesis, chapters 6 to 9). Give a brief account of the Bible story of the Flood. What can historians tell us about the Flood and its effects on the early Sumerians? Find out about King Ur-Nammu and the third dynasty at Ur.
3. Describe the Sumerians' weaving, farming, use of stone and metal.
4. Describe the discovery of the wheel and the arch, and the use made of them by the Sumerians. What is the importance of these discoveries?
5. Describe and give an example of Sumerian art. Describe Sumerian education and compare it with our school.
6. Describe the Sumerian houses. What were their living conditions like? Draw a picture to illustrate your description. Compare a Sumerian house with the house or flat in which you live.
7. What is a slave? Did the Sumerians have slaves? How did they obtain slaves? What were the duties of a slave? Do we have slavery in England today?
8. How did the Sumerians write? Why is their writing called 'Cuneiform'? Compare their writing with the writing we use in England today.
9. What gods did the Sumerians worship? What were their temples like? Draw a picture of a Ziggurat. Draw a picture of our parish church and compare it with a Sumerian temple.
10. What trade did the Sumerians have? How did they carry goods they wished to trade? What methods of transport have we today for trade? Where did the Sumerians trade? What goods did they carry?

Use your own words for the descriptions you give – do not just copy from the book.
Use illustratious, diagrams and maps wherever you think they will help.

Books which will help you:
Richard Carrington: *Ancient Sumer*
Museum Bookshelf *Ancient Civilizations*, book 2.
Marie Neurath and Evelyn Worboys: *They lived like this in Ancient Mesopotamia*
Oxford Junior Encyclopaedia

Lessons 5–9: Project work
Pupils work largely on their own. Teacher acts as a consultant.

Lessons 10–12: Discussion of project work
Purpose to draw the threads of the three projects together. The projects could be taken separately and pupils could describe various aspects of the work. The last part of the third lesson could be spent as a free movement 'museum period' in which the pupils could examine and discuss the displayed material.

Second year

Two forty-minute lessons a week
Term one: 12 lessons

THE REFORMATION

Lesson 1: Exposition, questioning, discussion
Background to the reformation. Starting point: FID DEF on coins. This leads in to the religious controversy. Describe religious position in Italy (centre discussion on photographs of St. Peter's) and in Germany (Tetzel and indulgences makes a good story).

Lessons 2–4: Project work on Luther and Calvin
Each pupil to produce a short booklet. Assignment cards indicate the main points to be investigated and books to be consulted.

Lesson 5: Discussion of project work
Pupils describe and discuss aspects of the life of Luther and Calvin. Teacher expands or explains as necessary. Date chart of the two religious leaders' lives built up on the board and appended to the pupils' project work. Lutheranism and Calvinism abroad: the intolerance of the new religions.

Lessons 6–7: Play reading and discussion
Act I, 'The Crucible', by Arthur Miller.
(Rather strong meat, perhaps, for second year pupils; but properly introduced and explained it could provide a powerful commentary on seventeenth-century Puritanism in Massachusetts).

Lesson 8: Filmstrip and discussion
'King Henry VIII': 215 G28 £1 0 0: a Common Ground filmstrip available from the Foundation Film Library, Brooklands House, Weybridge, Surrey. Select frames from the strip so that discussion can centre on: Henry VIII's character; his links with the renaissance; the story of the English Reformation.

Lessons 9–12: Project and field work on a local monastery
(A whole morning or afternoon will have to be set aside for the visit to the monastery).
Two lessons spent in preparation: setting the background; looking at photographs, maps and diagrams of the monastery; and organising the groups and their field work. Form to be divided into six groups, each assigned a different part of the monastery and grounds to investigate. For example:
Group 1: the church.
Group 2: the guest house, cellarium and cloister.
Group 3: the refectory, kitchens, dormitories.
Group 4: the chapter house, cells, infirmary.
Group 5: the manor house.
Group 6: the geographical position of the monastery.
Each group should produce diagrams of its area and sketch drawings.

In addition, each group should find specific information about the history of the monastery. Much of this work will be done in the classroom or for homework rather than during the expedition to the monastery.
Group 1: What was the order to which the monks belonged? Write a brief account of the order.
Group 2: How many monks were there in 1536? How many lay brothers? What property and land did the monastery own?
Group 3: When was the monastery built? Where did the material come from? Mention some of the differences in building styles between the various religious orders.
Group 4: Who were the chief officials in the monastery? What were the three vows taken by the monks? Give a brief description of a day in the life of a monk.
Group 5: Who bought the monastery after the dissolution? Give a brief account of the subsequent history of the monastery.
Group 6: What other religious houses were there in the district? Give a brief account together with a map.

The finished work can be mounted for display.

Third year

Two forty-minute lessons a week
Term one: 12 lessons

Lesson 1 : Exposition, questioning, discussion
Starting point: Waterloo. Read a brief eyewitness account of the battle (e.g. The Life Guard's letter given in *They saw it Happen, 1689–1897*, edited by T. Charles–Edwards and B. Richardson, Basil Blackwood, 1958, pp. 164–165). The end of a story and the beginning of a new era (cf. 1945). What sort of problems had the government to face? What type of government was in power? What form did the unrest take? What powers for keeping law and order had the government at its disposal ?

Lesson 2 : Examination of documents
Photostat copies of local newspapers (obtained from the local records office) describing disturbances between 1815 and 1832 issued to each pupil in the class. Paragraphs from the papers read and discussed. Introduce the subject of growing demand for parliamentary reform.

Lessons 3–5 : Project work
Project work on parliamentary reform – if possible with reference to local events. Each pupil to produce a short booklet. Assignment cards indicate the main points to be investigated and books to be consulted.

Lesson 6 : Discussion of project work
Pupils describe and discuss their project work. Teacher explains or expands as necessary.

Lessons 7–12 : Project and field work: the growth of a local town in the nineteenth century
Introductory period: the national background; the growth of paternalism in government; extension of powers of local authorities. Industrialism and the growth of towns.
Group work (both in classroom and town) leading to a display:
Group 1: Population changes 1800 – 1960 and increase in housing (through local maps). One street could be analysed to show changes in building style.
Group 2: The road system in 1800 and today. A traffic census could be taken.
Group 3: Local government: how it works in the borough. The historical background.
Group 4: The railway: when it was built; its effect on the town.
Group 5: Local industry: when it was established; numbers employed.
Group 6: Occupations at the beginning of the nineteenth century. Survey of sample of male population today: where they work; how they go to work.

Groups should work as individual units; two groups could be out on field work unsupervised while the rest of the class works at school. The project should end with a general pooling of information.
   The organisation of these lessons needs great care and will to a large

extent be governed by the particular local situation. Because of this only the briefest indication is given of the lessons. It could be that more than six will be required; it will depend on the enthusiasm of the pupils, the nature of the material available and, indeed, the general success of the project.

Some teachers, of course, may have the opportunity to take their pupils to a local authority residential centre where the running of such schemes in many ways is an easier matter. Pupils stay for a period of about a week and follow a course of environmental studies. In the area in which the enquiry was undertaken, Southampton Education Committee's Summer School at Stubbington, for example, is set in an area rich with possibilities for historical field work, and the writer knows of several history teachers who have run enterprising and successful projects from this centre. Information about residential centres can be obtained from local authorities. Teachers who are looking for specific guidance about the organisation of historical field work will find a number of useful books.

For example:

M. BERESFORD, *History on the Ground*, Lutterworth, 1957

FRANCIS CELORIA, *Local History*, English Universities Press, Teach Yourself Series, 1958

R. DOUCH, *Local History and the Teacher*, Routledge & Kegan Paul, 1967

F. G. EMMISON, *Archives and Local History*, Methuen, 1966

W. G. HOSKINS, *Local History in England*, Longmans, 1959

W. E. TATE, *The Parish Chest: a study of the records of parochial administration*, Cambridge University Press, 1951

JOHN WEST, *History Here and Now*, Schoolmaster Publishing Co., 1966

Finally, though intended primarily for the geographer, the history teacher can learn much from:

MARGARET S. DILKE, ed., *Field Studies for Schools*, Vol. 1: *The Purpose and Organization of Field Studies*. Vol. 2: *Field Excursions in the North West of England*, Rivington, 1965

Fourth and fifth years

Four forty-minute lessons a week
Term three: 12 lessons

RUSSIA AND THE 1917 REVOLUTION

These lessons are designed for pupils entered for either the C S E or G C E examinations. Most teachers will feel that with examination forms notes must play some part. It is suggested that pupils' notes, whether individually made or issued, should be kept in a ring file. Project booklets can also be inserted. Exercise books can then be reserved for essays and short pieces of written work.

Teachers will find the Historical Association's 'Teaching of History' booklet no. 4 very useful for this series of lessons: *Russia – Notes on a*

Course for Secondary Schools, compiled by P. D. Whitting, Historical Association, rev. edn, 1966.

Lessons 1 – 2 : Exposition, questioning, discussion
Introduction: Russia today. Its geography and immense size: implications strategically. The ancien regime: Tartars; Peter the Great; serfdom. Backwardness of the country in 1900; immense gulf between rich and poor; the beginnings of industrialisation. Musical illustration and, more obviously, pictorial illustration could be used effectively here. Filmstrips, photographs, posters and maps can be borrowed free of charge (postage must be refunded) from The Society for Cultural Relations with the U S S R, 118 Tottenham Court Road, London W.1.

Lesson 3 : Preparation for lectures and discussion
Brief introduction to Marx and Lenin. Remainder of period spent by the pupils preparing lectures on the two men. Principal points to be investigated should be listed on the board.

Lesson 4 : Lectures and discussion
Brief lectures from one or two of the pupils on the work done in the previous lesson. Discussion. Teacher introduces topic for the next lesson – the 1905 revolution.

Lessons 5–6 : Newspapers
Each pupil to produce a newspaper supposed to have been printed the day after 'Bloody Sunday'. The newspaper should be made on unlined paper, about 2 ft. by 1 ft. 6 in. Principal points to be included (for example, the social, political and industrial background to the revolution; the Russo-Japanese war; the immediate causes) to be listed on the board; but pupils should be encouraged to adopt a pro-government or pro-worker attitude. Illustrations and maps should be included. The finished newspapers can be displayed in the history room.

Lessons 7–8 : Film and discussion (double lesson required).
'Battleship Potemkin', available from Contemporary Films Ltd., 14 Soho Square, London W.1. Duration 70 minutes, cost of hire £3 10s. Extra time will have to be made for general discussion.

Lessons 9–11 : Project work
The causes and course of the 1917 revolution. Individual booklets to be produced by each pupil. Assignment cards indicate the main points to be investigated and books to be consulted. The information should be set against a date chart. Illustrations and maps should be encouraged.

Lesson 12 : Discussion of project work
Pupils describe and discuss their work. At the end of the lesson, duplicated notes could be issued which cover the twelve lessons.

4 The construction and marking of the history tests

The problems of syllabus, techniques and aims lead to those of assessment, for we must be concerned not only with what, how and why we teach but also with the extent to which our objectives have been achieved. Assessment procedures, of course, can assume several forms. The most obvious (and perhaps most valuable) is the broad, unspecified assessment of the pupil's progress and development with which the able teacher is constantly concerned, and which forms the hallmark of any valid teaching situation. Then there is the recorded continuous assessment of work pursued over a period of time; and closely allied with this the assessment of a project or personal topic. Finally, there are the various types of test papers – written examinations which the candidate has to answer within a given time limit. It is with this aspect of assessment that the remainder of this book is concerned. The chapters present and discuss the history tests constructed for this investigation – tests which were designed partly to investigate new ways of examining, partly to explore the nature of the pupils' knowledge of history. The first is the concern of this chapter which describes the construction of the tests and their marking scheme. In the following chapter the pupils' written answers and their subsequent spoken comments are discussed. Such description and discussion, however, are given greater sharpness when set against the philosophical background which helped to shape the tests and the assessment procedures; and the opening paragraphs of this chapter attempt to make explicit a personal philosophy which has perhaps been implicit in much that has already been written.

It is of course questionable whether we need any sort of formal written examination in history at the end of the fourth or fifth year in the secondary school. Some might feel that continuous assessment and topic work (which can play an important part in CSE schemes) give a fuller and more satisfactory picture of the pupil's achievement than any history paper – particularly as it seems as though many of the present external examinations are no more than tests of fragments of knowledge whose influence extends beyond the examination room and affects the quality and emphasis of the teacher's classroom practice.

Yet good examinations – examinations that really deal with the aims of history teaching – have a part to play in our profession, a part that cannot be superseded entirely by continuous assessment or personal topic work. There is no need to rehearse the obvious arguments – the incentive to pupils, the chance of comparing performances and so on; but from the teacher's point of view it is surely important to be able not only to assess

D

the extent to which pupils have achieved the objectives set out but also to diagnose deficiences or misunderstandings. Though we are doing this in some degree continuously, the task of setting an examination should force us to concentrate on the particular problems of the philosophy and objectives of our teaching; and the test itself should provide a valid and reliable measuring instrument.

Two assumptions underlie this statement: first, that the construction and assessment of the examination is teacher controlled – an assumption which is inherent in the philosophy of C S E; secondly, that history examinations which adequately measure the aims we seek to teach can be devised and reliably assessed. The senior teachers made clear that their objectives go far beyond the mere accumulation of data; that they are concerned with the mental skills of understanding and evaluation and with the emotional responses of receiving and sympathising. Most history teachers would subscribe to this view and are anxious to use assessment procedures which are designed to measure at least some of these aims. Much current educational research has been concerned with the problems of valid test construction but little of this work has dealt with the particular problems of assessment in history. While Nuffield science, English and language projects, for example, are changing the form and purpose of testing in these subjects, there has been little change in the pattern of written history examinations, which remain much as they were in the late nineteenth century when large-scale public examining was first established. But there is a growing feeling that history too must undergo a reconsideration; and there is an increasing demand for a new type of test which takes more account of the understandings and attitudes with which we are concerned.

One general attempt to solve this problem has been made recently by a committee of American college and university examiners; and their two publications which they call the *Taxonomy of Educational Objectives*[1] have helped to clarify the aims of the curriculum and to suggest ways of measuring in all subjects a range of mental and emotional behaviours. Taxonomies, classifications into categories, are an indispensible part, for example, of the biologist's work: they enable him to speak a language common to all biologists. What the American examiners have attempted to do is to build up a classification of educational objectives, a framework within which the aims of every field of study can be expressed. It was hoped that this would enable subject aims to be expressed with more precision and allow searching and accurate assessment to be undertaken. The *Taxonomy* looks at behaviour in three major parts: the cognitive, the affective and the psychomotor. The cognitive deals with the thinking processes – recall and recognition situations and intellectual abilities and skills; *Handbook 2* is concerned with attitudes, values and interests. The third domain is the one which deals with the manipulative and motor

[1] B. Bloom *et al*, eds, *Taxonomy of Education Objectives*: *Handbook 1: the Cognitive Domain*; *Handbook 2: the Affective Domain*, English editions, Longmans, 1965.

84

skills; as yet no publication has been produced by the committee. Within the cognitive and affective domain objectives are broken down, classified and numbered according to the decimal classification system. Thus the cognitive domain starts with 1.0, Knowledge, subdivided into 1.10, Knowledge of specifics; 1.20, Knowledge of ways and means of dealing with specifics; 1.30, Knowledge of universals and abstractions in a field. It moves on to look at the intellectual abilities and skills, that is, ways of using the discrete pieces of information given in the first category. Thus 2.0 is Comprehension; 3.0, Application; 4.0, Analysis; 5.0, Synthesis; 6.0, Evaluation – each of these having subdivisions (for example, 2.10, Translation; 2.20, Interpretation; 2.30, Extrapolation). The affective domain starts with the simplest of attitudes, 1.0, Receiving, and progresses through 2.0, Responding, 3.0, Valuing, 4.0, Organisation to 5.0, Characterisation by a value or value complex.

This attempt to cut away the woolliness of language which often characterises both teachers and educationists when they come to talk of aims and objectives must be welcomed. The examples given at the ends of the two handbooks of the ways in which the various objectives can be assessed are interesting and make a welcome break with the time honoured examination methods with which teachers are only too familiar.

Some educationists, however, have had reservations about the *Taxonomy*'s division of human behaviour into the cognitive and affective domains. The difficulties of such a division were recognised by the committee, and in *Handbook 2* frequent reference is made to the ways in which affective and cognitive behaviours intertwine and overlap. Yet, the argument goes, for the sake of clarity the two must be considered separately. It is, however, questionable whether any test or teaching situation can be devised in which thought and emotion are kept apart. The pupil is not just a thinking individual or an emotional being but an infinitely complex mixture of both; and as teachers surely our concern must be with wholeness of personality and not with attempts at dissection which would destroy humanity's essential texture. More than this, the hierarchy of cognitive abilities which the *Taxonomy* postulates bears little resemblance to the actual ways in which learning takes place in history; for example, many of the higher cognitive categories will often be interwoven with the recall and recognition situations of the first category. In any case, child psychologists such as Piaget, who have analysed the development and structure of children's thinking, have shown that the pupil's mental processes are certainly more complicated and perhaps more beautiful than the cognitive taxonomy would suggest.

But the importance of the *Taxonomy* lies in its emphasis on the emotional as well as the mental outcomes of learning – or to use G. H. Bantock's words that the syllabus should bring 'self-realisation through self-transcendence';[1] and though the committee's attempts to particularise this behaviour and to suggest ways of measuring it have not been altogether

[1] G. H. Bantock, *Education in an Industrial Society*, Faber, 1963, p. 172.

successful, the *Taxonomy* is a useful starting point for the re-evaluation of examining techniques in history.

The *Taxonomy* provided a directive for the construction and marking of the history tests which were drawn up for this investigation. The classification's emphasis on the emotional and mental use that can be made of basic data prompted the formulation of questions which ask for the comprehension, analysis and valuing of historical knowledge, and not merely the unintelligent regurgitation of facts.

What then were the criteria on which the selection of material for the tests was based? Inevitably they must be founded on some fairly clear philosophy, for the very act of selection, the words used, the kind of answers expected from the pupils, presupposes a framework, a set of references. The starting point for the construction of the tests was that essential element of history – time. Though chronological or developmental history should not be taught to pupils (an argument that has been advanced in chapter 2), no teacher can deny the importance of the concept of time in shaping his own interpretation and understanding of the subject. The ancient historians such as Thucydides or Polybius considered history to be a series of recurring cycles, and wrote their works from this point of view. Today we think of historical time in linear terms; and though there is disagreement as to its exact nature, all would accept the view that it is an irreversible process, and that the accurate dating of events in terms of the time scale is an important part of the historian's task.

Historical time, however, is not a broad, even-flowing river on which all society is carried; such a concept does violence to the subtlety and texture of history. There are periods of change and periods of stagnation; teachers stress epochs such as the Renaissance, Reformation or Industrial Revolution because they were eras when society was radically and, in some instances, violently altered, when the tempo of life accelerated and its molecular structure increased in heat and movement. This analogy with a molecular structure is apt – for just as the movements of the minute parts differ in speed, so within the period of change the component parts of society are affected to a greater or lesser extent. Historical time is restless, uneven and as changeable as the sea; but inexorably it moves on, never to retrace its steps.

Of course, history is not concerned with time alone but with man in time and space. Man is the product of the past and stands in direct relationship to it; the past is part of his very being. Thus history exists as the collective experience of mankind, just as the history of an individual forms his collective present; or to use the Italian philosopher Croce's paradox, 'All history is contemporary history'.

This notion of historical thinking as 'present thought' which lies behind Croce's philosophy and finds echoes in Collingwood's writing, gives history an immediacy and relevance which is of particular value to the teacher. If we see history as something which 'is', that is, 'has reality', then our task is not so much one of creating aims extrinsic to the subject but of introducing or initiating the pupil to history so that it impinges on his consciousness and is part of his experience, not in order that he may be a better citizen or more cosmopolitan in his outlook (though, indeed, these may be outcomes), but that he may become more truly himself; that he may establish a reflective relationship with the world of space, and man.

The achievement of this reflective relationship is what the Catholic priest Teilhard de Chardin has termed the process of 'hominisation' – man becoming truly man. This process he traces in *The Phenomenon of Man*, which discusses the evolution of the whole of prehuman, human, terrestial and cosmic experience. De Chardin argues that we are now reaching a new point where the 'penetrating and synthetic power of our gaze' is becoming conscious of the very process of our own evolution. This opens up great possibilities for mankind – possibilities of controlling and shaping our future destiny. Man, writes de Chardin, has the choice: 'to see or perish is the very condition laid upon everything that makes up the universe'. Nor must our seeing be a dispassionate appraisal but a fullblooded possession of the quality of life that encircles the earth. We are part of past experience, not outside it; the future lies in our control; and we must excercise all our faculties to perceive, grasp and possess this understanding.

It is one thing to consider and formulate a philosophy of history, another to make practical use of such beliefs. But this is what the teaching situation demands; and though there is the danger of bathos in moving from the heights of philosophy to the more mundane levels of the details of test construction, yet the philosophy is the mainspring of action, even if its influence is not always apparent. The selection of material for the tests therefore stems from the philosophy outlined above – a concept of humanity which emphasises its purposefulness and its cohesion, and therefore asserts the existence, in theory at any rate, of a Universal History. These beliefs show themselves throughout the test papers in the emphasis on the developing awareness of mankind and the structure of life, and in the questions which look for the pupils' sensitivity to the material they are given. This philosophy was limited by two obvious factors: first, the time/place frameworks which enclose the syllabuses of the schools; and secondly, the aspects of these periods which are stressed. There is, however, enough common ground between the schools to allow papers to be set which all the pupils should have had equal chance of answering; and the questions were based on major problems in history which are dealt with in some way by all five schools.

Paper I[1] asks the pupils to think about the fundamental quality of history – time and change – which marks it out as a discipline distinct from, say, English, sociology and geography (a trio with which, of course, it has much in common). The first two questions are concerned with the time relationship of events one to another and on a linear basis; the third asks about the effects of time – the changes the pupil thinks of as his mind ranges over the centuries. The intention of these questions therefore was

[1] The three research history test papers are given in Appendix VI, pp. 171–178.

to find out how far the developmental syllabus conveys a coherent, total picture. The changes inventions have made to our way of life, and the idea of rapid or revolutionary change, are the themes of the next three questions. What is the common element which allows both the industrial changes in England and the violent upheaval in France of the eighteenth century to be called 'revolutions'? Are the pupils able to think of other periods that can be similarly named? The British industrial revolution is a topic covered by all the schools: why was Britain the first country in the world to industrialise? When did other countries start making the sometimes painful change from an agricultural and land holding to an industrial and wage earning economy? In question 7 (see p. 173) the pupils fill in the table with the most appropriate countries from the list given. Other questions deal with population increases: the pupils have to think about birth and death rates, standards of living, emigration. Or, again, does a large population necessarily mean a powerful military nation? Is God always on the side of the big battalions? The final question of this paper looks at the standards of living and make pupils compare the financial lot of a worker in the early nineteenth century with that of a modern wage earner.

'Government, world affairs and our homes' is the theme of paper II. Politics are dealt with in the first two sections. The pupils have to consider three familiar political figures and say what, if anything, they have in common; and in the following section they compare the Peterloo episode with the 1926 general strike. The abandonment of a Eurocentric vision underlies the questions on social and cultural areas in 1450; and the world map was drawn with the Pacific and not the Atlantic as the principal ocean and little Europe out on a limb. With familiar material rearranged in this manner, how do the pupils react? How do they regard other civilisations about which they have learned? In short, what insights has the teaching of topics on European civilisation achieved? The final section deals with man and society from the domestic point of view. Photographs of houses were chosen to show different materials and techniques; but the buildings are of comparable size and attractiveness so that there should be no bias. The photograph of ribbon development (not strictly speaking 'classic' ribbon development for the areas behind the main road have been built on) was included so that pupils should be given the opportunity to compare and contrast sixteenth-century Mill street with some twentieth-century housing.

Paper III deals mainly with attitudes, ideas, beliefs. Confronted with three striking religious buildings of widely separated periods, what reactions do the pupils have? Do they sense any feeling of change or development in man's attitude to the unknown? Can they express this in words? A verse from the 'Song of Roland' (translation D. L. Sayers) makes a vivid contrast with part of Owen's well-known 'Dulce et decorum est'. Here it was hoped that the pupils would range freely outside the wording of the poems and explain the contrast in historical terms; and section three, the comparison of two extracts on London in the sixteenth and nineteenth centuries, had a similar purpose. The passages were chosen because they capture the spirit of the centuries in which they were written. The first comes from Paul Heutzner's *A Journey into England in the Year 1598*, the second from Taine's *Notes on England*. Finally a passage from George Fox's *Journal* is contrasted with an extract from *Breaking the Silence* by W. J. Weatherby; the pupils are confronted with the problems of intolerance but made to think of its positive and negative aspects.

It should be apparent that the three papers range fairly freely over the field of history. Essentially, it was hoped to avoid tests which concentrate on the factual content of a limited period. What is of interest is that when an analysis of the pupils' marks in the research history tests was made, it was found that though differences between the syllabuses and teaching methods were reflected in the scores for papers I and II, they were not reflected in those for paper III. Here it would seem that the pupils' historical ability was largely homogeneous. In other words, paper III, which above all required answers based on historical understanding rather than historical information, was the one least influenced by the different history courses of the schools. In so far as freedom of syllabus and method are desirable, the results of this broadly based examination have considerable significance for the history teacher. For the use of similar papers could mean that classroom practice need no longer be determined by the detailed requirements of a particular syllabus; and the pupils' performance in the examination is less likely to be influenced by either the 'luck of the draw' or the teacher's ability to predict the topics that will turn up.

This claim is dependent not only upon the philosophical argument but also on the reliability with which such examinations can be assessed; for unless consistency of marking can be achieved the examination will have little value. For this reason a fairly detailed discussion of the marking scheme adopted for the three papers is essential.

THE MARKING SCHEME

The answers in the research history tests fall into one of two marking categories. First, there are those which can be marked in a clearly objective manner – that is, where certain precise rules can be laid down which can be applied with complete reliability; secondly, those which are loosely and rather inaccurately called 'open-ended responses', that is, the form of the answer can vary considerably within the terms of the question, and must be assessed 'subjectively'.

Items in the first category are such that standard objective marking procedures are not applicable. In questions 1A and B, paper 1, for example, where events have to be placed in correct order of time, there are degrees of inaccuracy which must be taken into account when assessing the pupil's answer. This was done by correlating the pupil's order of events with the correct order. Readers who are familiar with this statistical procedure will,

I hope, forgive a brief explanation. A correlation is a measure of agreement between, for example, two sets of test scores. The coefficients range from $+1$ denoting complete agreement, through 0 denoting no agreement, to -1 denoting complete disagreement. Thus:

$$-1 \rule{3cm}{0.4pt} 0 \rule{3cm}{0.4pt} +1$$

-1 and $+1$, of course, represent the extreme ends of the scale and one seldom obtains coefficients which fall on these two points. The technique was applied to the 'time order' questions, for it gives a measure of comparison between the pupil's order and the correct order, and between the performance of one pupil and another, which is far more sensitive than either the crude right/wrong method of marking or the 'two marks, one mark, no marks' technique which is sometimes used. The correlation procedure takes account of the amount of inaccuracy and debits the score accordingly; the disadvantage of the method is that it is time consuming. An example may make the procedure clear.

Correct order	Pupil's order
1. Death of Socrates of Athens	1. Death of Socrates of Athens
2. First Crusade	3. Henry VIII of England's break with the R.C. Church.
3. Henry VIII of England's break with the R.C. Church.	2. First Crusade
4. American War of Independence	5. French Revolution.
5. French Revolution	4. American War of Independence
6. Year of your birth	7. Death of Stalin.
7. Death of Stalin	6. Year of your birth

Correct order	Pupils' order	C O deviations from mid point	P O deviations from mid point	C O deviations squared	C O deviations multiplied by P O deviations
1	1	-3	-3	$+9$	$+9$
2	3	-2	-1	$+4$	$+2$
3	2	-1	-2	$+1$	$+2$
4 mid point	5	0	$+1$	0	0
5	4	$+1$	0	$+1$	0
6	7	$+2$	$+3$	$+4$	$+6$
7	6	$+3$	$+2$	$+9$	$+6$
				$+28$	$+25$

Coefficient of correlation $= \dfrac{+25}{+28}$

The 'scores' obtained by this method can then be scaled as required.

Question 7, paper I, on the order of industrialisation of countries was marked in a similar way. However, the list at the top of the table contains more countries than there are places on the ladder and either Germany or U S A can correctly be put in position two: a variation had to be made. For convenience, France was 1, Germany and the U S A 2, Russia 3 and Communist China 5. The pupil's order was correlated with 1, 2, 3, 4, and 5 (India, number 4, was retained for the correlation in order to have an odd number of items; an odd number of places gives a midpoint which is a whole number, obviously easier to work with). Where there were two 2s adjacent (that is, where a pupil had included both the U S A and Germany on the ladder), or where there were two 2s, one of which fell on position 3, one mark was deducted from the score obtained from the correlation. Where the order was 2, 2, 3, 5 one mark was added to the score. Where two 2s were included but in neither of these positions, the final score was the one obtained from the correlation. In all cases the sums of the products of the deviations from the midpoint, 3, was regarded as the score – which in the case of five items is out of ten. An example will perhaps make this clear.

Correct order	Pupil's order	C O deviations from mid point	P O deviations from mid point	C O deviations squared	C O deviations multiplied by P O deviations
1	2	−2	−1	+4	+2
2	3	−1	0	+1	0
3 mid point	5	0	+2	0	0
4	4	+1	+1	+1	+1
5	2	+2	−1	+4	−2
				+10	+1

Score for the question: +1 out of +10

Once again, the scores can then be scaled.

Question 2, paper I (the linear position of events see p. 172) was marked in the following way. A cardboard ruler was made, along one edge of which was marked the hundred-year intervals of the question line and the correct positions of the ten events. A pupil's point which fell within fifteen years, plus or minus, of the correct position scored 5 marks; within thirty years, 4 marks, forty-five years, 3 marks and so on. The answers could be assessed quickly and accurately for the ruler had the score intervals marked and it was simply a case of positioning the ruler against the pupil's line and assessing the extent of the deviation of his points from the correct positions.

Marks for the dating of the two passages (questions a and b section three, paper III) were given on the following basis. For extract A, any date between 1550 and 1650 scored one mark; for extract B, any date between 1850 and 1914. The dates were adhered to rigidly, so that a pupil putting, for example, '1545' would not score. 'Late 16th century', 'early 17th century', 'late 19th century' and 'early 20th century' were accepted.

Most of the questions, however, require sentence or paragraph answers, and a rather more lengthy discussion is needed to describe the scheme that was adopted for these. The 'one point, one mark' scheme which determines much of the assessment of continuous prose answers in history was rejected outright. Such an approach not only tends to overlook the thought processes of the candidate but puts excessive premium on the memorisation of discrete pieces of information. By concentrating on the 'parts', we lose sight of the 'whole' or 'gestalt'. On the other hand, the impression marking which has been used successfully with English essays[1] does not seem directly applicable to history. In English when the pupil has to write an essay on 'The County Fair' or similar subject, the freedom of expression, style and content is great, the principal limiting factors being the rules of English grammar and spelling – for some pupils not even that. In history the pupil who is asked to comment on photographs or extracts, for example, has somewhat smaller room for manoeuvre. Though obviously imaginative effort must play an important (or perhaps the chief) part, his argument must be relevant to the material, and he must operate within an historical framework. A first reading of the completed tests, therefore, showed two things. First, that the pupils had treated the questions demanding sentence and paragraph answers in very varying ways; but that, secondly, these answers tended to group themselves. From this impression a scheme for classifying the written work was evolved.

Three basic categories were used. Responses which showed:
1. powers of selection, of critical thinking, and above all the ability to work relevantly outside the given material but within an historical framework were assigned to category H (= historical understanding).
2. comprehension and intelligent handling of the material, but which made little or no attempt to draw on historical material or understandings outside the question, were assigned to category PC (= précis comprehension).
3. little real comprehension of the material or question and which made no attempt to expand or apply any information given were assigned to category PNC (= précis non-comprehension).

The three main categories were subdivided: this helped to sharpen the results by increasing the discrimination. Category PC1/H3 was reserved for responses which showed the glimmers of historical understanding but were not worthy of full inclusion in the H category. Conversion to a 10 or 5

[1] For example: Schools Council: *Multiple Marking of English Compositions*, Examinations Bulletin No. 12, H.M.S.O., London, 1966.

point scale could then be effected. The table below shows the gradings and their numerical equivalents.

Table 5. Marking categories: 'subjective' items, research history tests

	Category	10 point scale	5 point scale
	H1	10	5
H	H2	9	
	H3	8	4
PC1/H3		7	
	PC1	6	3
PC	PC2	5	
	PC3	4	2
	PNC1	3	
PNC	PNC2	2	1
	PNC3	1	0

Such a scale is hardly original – after all, most of us think in this manner when we are marking homework. However, it is believed that such a formal scheme has not been used for the marking of a history examination. Its merit is that it looks at the quality and not the quantity of thought, and this makes it perfectly possible to use it to grade single sentence, paragraph or essay answers.

To test the reliability of the classification scheme, the papers were assessed twice; once by the writer and once by a secondary school history teacher of many years' experience. Three examples are given of the way in which it was applied.

Question 8, paper I, is one of these which required what may loosely be described as a factual answer. It asks: 'Write *two* sentences each giving *one* reason why Britain was the first country in the world to undergo the industrial revolution?'

This is how a girl answered the question:

'Britain was a rich country and could afford to start industries. There was also available coal for the industries.'

The first marker (the writer) graded this H2, the second, H3. The answer shows a clear historical understanding of the economic state of Britain in the eighteenth century and of the raw material available; it hardly qualifies for the top category for there is no mention of the trade and wool industry on which this wealth was largely based, nor of the other raw materials which were to play such an important part in Britain's industrial expansion.

The next pupil was graded PC2 by both markers. She wrote:

'Because the British were the first to invent the means of power to drive machines instead of using manpower which was slower and more costly. Also the British were easily supplied with coal for steam and wool which was the main beginnings of British Industry.'

The pupil understands the question and has made an intelligent attempt to answer it; but her response puts the cart before the horse. She does not explain why Britain should have been in a position to develop steam power, though the last sentence implies that she sees some connection with the national coal fields. She makes a reference to the wool trade but is unsure about the part it played in the growth of industry. She is not in fact showing any great awareness of the structure of Britain at that time, and has merely picked on one or two important factors.

A boy from Benborough (with an I Q of 143) could only think of one point; he wrote:

> 'After the Romans had left Britain, British people know what luxuries could be had but it took time before the knowledge could be used to obtain pleasures.'

This reveals a curious reasoning; it is almost as though he had tried to be too clever. It shows a complete lack of understanding of the social, political or economic structure of eighteenth-century Britain – or rather a by-passing of these aspects. Instead, his thought process seems to have worked in this manner: 'Industrialisation means a rising standard of living which brings greater comfort, something I know everyone today is clamouring for. Obviously Britain started to industrialise because she wanted higher wages. But why in the eighteenth century? Ah yes – the Romans with their civilisation (=a high standard of living) left Britain about then – rather like when American aid is withdrawn; and so the British felt the pinch and began to work hard.' He seems to have forgotten the fact that the question asks why Britain was the first, and that Roman occupation was not confined to Britain. It is, incidentally, worth noting here that this boy did poorly in the 'time questions' in paper I. Needless to say both markers graded his response 'PNC3'.

Question 5, paper I, is more broadly based and calls for more general historical understandings. No answer warranted an H1 grade but a boy was given grade H2 by the first marker, grade H3 by the second for the following response:

> 'A revolution is a drastic change (concerning countries) in the way of life of the population. The French revolution resulted in change in the rule of France, and the industrial revolution resulted in a change of people's way of life, by quickening communications and making them richer.'

He shows evidence here of extracting the common element and thinking about the nature of the events in an historical way: he studies the change in rule, communications, wealth. The answer can be put in the 'H' category. On the other hand, it is a little repetitive and clumsy and the cliché 'way of life' is not helpful; the writer felt that H2 was the correct subcategory for the response.

A Fairport boy was given a grade of PC2 by both markers for this answer.

> 'Features which have changed the normal person. In France the

fighting brought a new type of rule and in England a new type of everyday life at work.'

There is some comprehension of the changes involved: PC is the appropriate main category in which to put it. However, there has been little attempt to expand the nature of the change and there is little evidence that the boy has drawn on any historical understandings.

The following example from an N G S pupil was given a PNC3 grading by both markers.

'Revolutions are normally disagreements between Government and ordinary people and they cause the people to rebel and rise up against their government because of this disagreement.'

The answer has little to do with the question, it fails to see any connection between the two events and shows no evidence of historical understanding. The boy has obviously made no attempt to think about the meaning of the word 'revolution' in those contexts and merely jotted down the first explanation he could think of.

Section three, paper III (see p. 179), based on the two extracts from accounts of visits to London in 1598 and 1871, requires a paragraph answer and looks for broad historical knowledge.

A Fairport boy wrote (having dated the passages 1550 and 1880):

'A likes the city very much. B hates it. A is mainly concerned with the city itself and mentions the death of thirty men without any regret. Also, at this time, London has not suffered the industrial revolution. B is concerned about the inhabitants of the city and their lives. London is at this period suffering from jerry built get-rich-quickly building of wharves, warehouses, factories and the vast number of shoddy houses to accommodate the workers.'

This is quite well written. His explanation is based on sound historical argument and he has drawn on information outside the given material. His answer shows a nice appreciation of the wakening of social conscience which is taking place in the nineteenth century ('A . . . mentions the death of thirty men without any regret. . . . B is concerned about the inhabitants of the city and their lives'). Both markers put this in category H2.

The following answer was placed in category PC2 (she had dated the passages 1400 and 1880).

'The first writer approves of London but the second cannot think of anything to commend it.

The first writer is thinking of London from an outsider's point of view, he doesn't have to live there and therefore does not notice the rottenness of the place. The writer also wrote before the next and London was not then so dreary and overcrowded.

The second writer can only see filth and fog everywhere but in the second paragraph it shows that there are many more people who live in the streets.'

Such an answer is literary rather than historical and her explanation of the contrast is mainly in terms of the attitudes of the visitors rather than the changes which have occurred in London during the four hundred year period – though she does mention as an afterthought that the first writer 'wrote before the next and London was not then so dreary and over-crowded'.

The markers had little hesitation in placing the following answer in category PN3.

'The writer in the first extract approved of London the writer of the second did not. The writer in the first is admiring the buildings, the way and where they are built. He has enjoyed visiting London and seeing places of interest. He describes the better parts of London, the places that he enjoyed visiting. The writer in the second extract has decided that he dislikes London and can find nothing to complimentary to say about it. He criticises the buildings which are grimy and the children and men from the slum areas.'

She considered that the passages were written in 1500 and 1900.

There is no attempt here at explanation of the differences of attitude, and not the smallest indication that the pupil has thought about the changes that have taken place. She has done little more than précis a few pieces of information taken from the given material.

THE DOUBLE MARKING: EXTENT OF AGREEMENT BETWEEN MARKERS

The examples of the way in which the marking scheme was applied perhaps give the impression that the assignment of grades was always a clearcut matter. It was, indeed, fairly easy to decide into which of the three main categories an answer should be put; more difficult to choose between, for example, a PC2 and PC3 grade answer. If these difficulties had been too great, the original prerequisite of reliability could not have been met. In fact, however, the agreement between the two markers was enough to dispel original doubts as to the consistency of the marking.

The extent of this agreement was determined by calculating coefficients of correlation (the term is discussed on p. 90). While absolute judgments cannot be based on the coefficients obtained, this statistical method enables comparisons to be made. For example, it is possible to compare the consistency of the double marking between papers or to make comparisons with multiple markings of other tests. Analysis of the research history tests over the whole sample (that is, all three papers taken together) produced a correlation of over $+0.90$. Obviously putting all the marks together tends to lessen the differences between markers – discrepancies tend to compensate for each other; but if the amount of agreement between the two markers on individual papers in each school is looked at, nowhere is there a coefficient of less than $+0.78$ and most are over $+0.90$. These results show a very high measure of agreement and indicate that the scheme can be applied reliably. The consistency of marking here compares extremely favourably with the reliability claimed for the multiple marking of English compositions reported in Examination Bulletin No. 12 (see above, p. 90).

The high level of marker compatibility in the history tests becomes even more apparent when the coefficients are compared with those obtained by correlating a double marking of English essays in research reported in the Schools Council Examination Bulletin No. 16.[1] The marking of 1007 essays by two markers produced a coefficient of just over $+0.6$, of 949 by two other markers a coefficient of $+0.4$. In both cases the scripts were assessed by experienced teachers who had discussed standards prior to the marking.

The significance of these results would be minimised if the particular circumstances of the investigation were irrelevant to the normal teaching situation. Research projects are often criticised for operating from ivory towers and taking little account of the strains and pressures with which teachers have to cope. However, the marking of the history test papers was based on the well established principle of discussion and exchange of reference scripts. The second marker was thoroughly conversant with the philosophy and intentions of the tests; and this is an essential prerequisite for the reliable use of the scheme. But the achievement of this is not impossible for teachers, and there seems every reason to suppose that the marking scheme could be operated in any history test situation.

CONCLUSION

The essence of the marking scheme for the 'subjective' items is that it persuades the marker to think in terms of the quality of the pupil's thinking – the totality rather than the parts of his thought process. Conversion to a numerical scale is a subsequent mechanical process which enables certain statistical tests to be made. These can indicate, for example, the extent to which separate questions in the papers effectively discriminate between the more and less able pupils; it will then be possible to exclude from subsequent examinations items which are unduly hard, unduly easy or those for which all pupils tend to get the same marks. An excellent, straightforward account of such procedures is given by D. R. Mather, N. France and G. T. Sare, in *The C S E: a handbook for moderators*, Collins, 1965. Examinations Bulletin No. 1 *The Certificate of Secondary Education: some suggestions for Teachers and Examiners*, H M S O London, 1963, also discusses simple statistical techniques which can be of value in analysing examination results. The purpose of this chapter, however, has been to show that valid tests of historical thinking can be constructed and reliably marked. The tests used were experimental; but the favourable results obtained might encourage the adoption of such examining, which in its turn could stimulate further trials along these lines.

[1] Schools Council: *The Certificate of Secondary Education: Trial Examinations: Written English*. Examinations Bulletin No. 16, H.M.S.O. London, 1967.

5 The pupils' historical thinking

The grading of the papers formed the background to the more detailed analysis of the quality and nature of the pupils' test answers. This chapter deals with two aspects of this analysis. First, it compares the pupils' performance in the general ability test (loosely, their intelligence quotients) with their history test scores. Secondly, it discusses the pupils' written and spoken answers to the history test material. Essentially, therefore, the following paragraphs bring together the various aspects of history teaching which so far have been dealt with separately; and the discussions under the headings of syllabus, techniques, objectives and assessment are merged to give a picture of their real interdependence.

THE PUPILS' I QS AND HISTORY TEST PERFORMANCE

When statistical comparison was made between the history test scores and the pupils' I Q s, it was found that there was little or no agreement; most of the co-efficients for the separate papers and ability test scores by schools are in the region of -0.3 to $+0.3$. These coefficients must be treated with caution. The school samples are small in size and homogeneous, factors which will tend to produce low correlations. However, the implications of the results are of interest, for it would seem that those pupils who do well in the conventional intelligence test do not necessarily perform successfully in a test of historical thinking. In other words, an interpretation of a pupil's intelligence in terms of his I Q alone may often overlook other intellectual abilities which the child possesses. Important and exciting research has been done in America and more recently in England by Dr L. Hudson[1] on the wider implications of this complex and subtle problem. Hudson distinguishes between pupils whom he calls 'convergers' and those he calls 'divergers'. The former have high I Qs, are able to deal with problems which have clearcut answers (on to which the mind can 'converge') and are frequently to be found studying science subjects. They tend, however, to show limited ability to think imaginatively or creatively. Divergers score low marks on I Q tests but show powers of imagination and verbal dexterity which the convergers lack; they enjoy tackling problems where the mind can 'diverge' – branch off and explore. They prefer arts subjects.

The correlations of the I Q scores with the research history tests give some support to this thesis; and empirically too the lack of agreement

[1] L. Hudson, *Contrary Imaginations: a psychological study of the English schoolboy*, Methuen, 1966.

between I Q and mental flexibility could be sensed. A specific example may help to make the point clear.

Gardiner is a quiet, thoughtful boy from Fairport grammar school, aged fifteen and a quarter. His sensitive comments have been quoted several times in the previous chapters, and he will be contributing to the following section. His I Q of 114 is well below the form mean of 126 and the sample mean of 129·4. His interests are sailing, cars, dogs, cycling and reading; he named two historical books he has recently read, *Sir Nigel* by Conan Doyle and *His was the Glory* by Styles. English is his best subject, art his worst; he hopes to study English, French, German or history in the sixth form. He would like to go to university or college after leaving school and wants to become a business executive. The topic he enjoyed learning about most in his first three years at secondary school was the Renaissance; he liked studying governmental development this year and disliked the classes spent on the Indian mutiny. On the first marker's assessment he scored the highest marks in each of the three tests. His answers combined succinctness with accuracy and understanding; and in the interviews he talked with remarkable fluency and insight about the problems the history papers had posed.

Compare Gardiner with Thomas, a Benborough pupil with an I Q of 143. He is a small and curious boy described by his form master as 'cunning rather than intelligent', and with an aptitude for poaching. Fishing and cricket are the only hobbies he noted on his questionnaire; he 'never' reads historical books; geography is his best, Latin his worst subject. He wants to read mathematics, chemistry and physics (and English, though it is difficult to see where this fits in) in the sixth form but is uncertain about his career beyond that. Rather surprisingly, he indicated that he likes history; the topic he enjoyed most both this year and over the past four years is the Crimean war. His marks in all of the history tests were below average; and in the interview he showed a stony obtuseness which was not merely churlishness.

It is perhaps too easy to label Gardiner a 'diverger', Thomas a 'converger', for it is impossible to say whether the disparity between their I Q scores and test and interview performance is due to innate mental dispositions or to the sort of history teaching they have received up to now. For example, Jollife and Brown (two potential scientists whose adverse comments on history were discussed at the end of the pupils' section in chapter 3) are very intelligent but did poorly in the research tests. Their poor performance is perhaps more a reflection of their outspoken dislike of history, and therefore their lack of interest in the history tests, than of their 'convergent' mentalities. Perhaps this lack of interest stems from their convergent bias? The investigation did not go far enough to establish an answer here, and all that can be tentatively suggested is that the teaching can play as big a part in creating disposition as any innate tendency.

It might be expected that pupils who performed well in one history paper would do equally well in the other two; to use statistical language, that the tests would show a high measure of correlation. Hudson, however, points out that 'One of the worst snags with the various tests of divergence is that they do not correlate well with each other. Getzels and Jackson quote correlations between open-ended tests of the order 0·3 – 0·4 and correlations between open-ended tests and an intelligence test of the order of 0·2 – 0·3,' (*op. cit.* p. 39). Strictly speaking, of course, the research history tests are not open-ended, for the answers must be based on an historical argument. Nevertheless, the intention when framing the questions was to make the pupils think historically in their own way, and because of this the tests have a certain affinity with those which are usually referred to as open-ended. Certainly correlations between the history tests seem to bear out Hudson's statement, for most of the coefficients are in the order of + 0·3 – that is, there was little consistency in the performance of the pupils between papers.

In conclusion, perhaps the fairest comment comes from Hudson himself: 'If you have before you a group of clever school children, a knowledge of their scores on an intelligence test will be of little help in guessing what their scores on an open-ended test will be. And a knowledge of their scores on one open-ended test will be of relatively little use in guessing their scores on another' (*op. cit.* p. 40).

The results of this investigation lend some weight to Hudson's view; they certainly show the dangers of thinking of intelligence in too limited terms, and emphasise the potentiality for divergent, creative thought in many of our 'less able' pupils. In the next section a less exact but possibly more revealing analysis of these divergent mental processes in history is undertaken.

THE PUPILS' TEST ANSWERS AND THE INTERVIEWS

The argument advanced in this section is straightforward: many pupils have a potential for divergent, imaginative thinking in history which our teaching often fails to stimulate. There is nothing very new or startling in this statement; practically every book or report on the teaching of history has raised the same point.[1] But this very repetition underlines the shortcomings of our present practice; and the doubts expressed by the teachers who helped in this research and the gloom showed by the pupils in their comments on history teaching find reflection in the children's test performance.

Only four aspects of the history tests are dealt with here: answers to questions on the British industrial revolution, standards of living, world history, photographs and extracts. Such a division excludes many questions and deals with some under one heading that could equally well have come under another. However, enough material is discussed to illustrate the

[1] For example: F. C. Happold, *The Approach to History*, London, Christophers, 1928, Introduction and preface; I.A.A.M., *The Teaching of History*, 3rd edn, Cambridge University Press, 1965, p. 63.

argument outlined above; and the anomalies the rigid treatment has created are the price that must be paid for clarity.

The pupils first touched on the British industrial revolution in question 3, paper I. This asked them to note four striking changes they would have seen in England had they been transported by time machine from the year A D 1066 to A D 1750. About a quarter of the pupils had seized on the date 1750 and equated it with a partly or fully industrial Britain. Several of this group considered this to be the most important change, and a Daymer girl's answer highlights a number of misconceptions about this period held by many of the pupils.

'The developments in industry would have been tremendous, having been landed in the midst of the industrial revolution. Great factories had taken over the work previously done in homes i.e. the making of cloth etc. Machinery had taken over from doing things by hand.'

A boy from Neil wrote in the same vein.

'I think No. 4 ('change in factories etc.') is the most significant because in 1750 machines and other means of manufacture were just being invented and hand made articles were all being made on these machines.'

This lack of understanding of a period all the pupils had studied came out more clearly in question 5, paper I, which asks about the features common to both the industrial and French revolutions. There was remarkably little feeling for the situation, a lack of ability to grasp its structure and quality. The following written answers are typical of the pupils' treatment of this question.

'In both these 'revolutions' the ultimate aim was for a better life for the people and more prosperity, in France it was for another gov., in England industry. Also they were both new ideas and came suddenly, spreading very quickly' (boy, B G S).

'In both periods the lower classes rebelled against the higher classes who ruled over them. They both were also violent and they did not just complain using words but took physical action' (D G S).

'They both happened suddenly and over a short period of time a lot changed' (F G S).

'The features common to these periods which allow us to call them revolutions are mainly concerned with change. In both these were quick and decisive changes for the better, this is true revolution' (N G S).

'The changes came abruptly. Peoples lives were affected and they took great parts in 'revolutions' (S G S).

The words 'change', 'improvement' and 'rapidly' occurred frequently, and the phrases 'lower classes', 'middle classes' were used freely and with little indication that their meaning was understood. Indeed, the data which they presented had all the appearances of externality which half digested clichés can give; and the following conversation is typical of the limited historical thinking created by this lack of contact with the period.

MB: Does the industrial revolution affect ordinary middle class sort of people – doctors, lawyers, teachers?

GIRL S G S: Well, I'd think it would affect them because they'd have people underneath them anyway.

MB: Can you think of any real reason? Did the transport system alter during the industrial revolution?

GIRL: Railways.

MB: In what ways would you say the coming of railways would alter the lives of ordinary middle class people? (pause) You don't think it would alter them in any way?

GIRL: No.

MB: My life has changed an awful lot now since I've got a motor car. In what ways has it changed?

GIRL: You can move around more quickly.

MB: Does this have any connection with the coming of railways?

GIRL: Yes – I see what you mean.

MB: Can you give me any definite ways in which the patterns of life within the family unit are going to be changed?

GIRL: Well, there's going to be a different way of doing things.

MB: For example, let's suppose the eldest son is going to get married. Before the coming of the railways, where would he probably have married?

GIRL: Near his home.

The clue to understanding came when a personal transport revolution, brought about through the purchase of a motor car, was linked with the coming of the railways; a credible event gave reality to a hypothetical situation. Thinking could proceed more purposefully because the topic had made contact.

Regression to intuitional thought showed itself clearly in question 8 ('Give two reasons why Britain was the first country in the world to industrialise') – the last of those dealing with the industrial revolution. Only seven pupils wrote answers which were considered worthy of category H. The majority were of the following calibre:

'It was the most highly populated country in relation to its size. Therefore it was in need of most industry to supply money and places for people to work in' (girl, B G S).

'Britain is small therefore it was easier to spread good ideas over a small area' (boy, B G S).

'Britain needed changes in industry. Britain had ideas' (D G S).

'We had all the inventors at the time – Trevithick, Murdoch, Watt, Boulton, and Stephenson. This was undoubtedly the reason for no other countries had such talent' (F G S).

'Because people had ideas about what should be done. Also Britain was thicker populated than most countries' (N G S).

'Britain's factories and machinery were becoming old fashioned and she would stick to her old traditions. She was producing for the home market rather than for the rewarding foreign market' (S G S).

This type of thinking continued to crop up in the interviews, and the pupils would time and again come out with statements such as these when asked to give a reason for Britain's lead in the industrial revolution:

'We didn't have so much agricultural land' (D G S);

'We had the brains, knowledge and intelligence', (D G S, F G S twice, N G S, S G S twice);

'We believed in education more' (N G S),

'It was an island and had to get on on its own', (girl, B G S),

'It needed it more', (F G S),

'People were more advanced and they realised they were getting a raw deal . . . they decided to create better conditions' (N G S),

and it seemed that intelligent pupils were jumping to illogical answers because they were unused to thinking round an historical problem of this nature. Again, the right question could sometimes put a pupil on to a more productive line of thought. A girl from Daymer had been graded PNC1 for this answer in the test:

'We needed to have better weaving and spinning mills to make cloths quicker for coats for our soldiers when we were fighting France. We also needed more ammunition factories so we could send our soldiers to fight France fully equipped for battle.'

The answer shows some understanding of the stimulation industry can receive from war – and, indeed, this girl was one of the few pupils who could see a connection between the two; but she has failed to deal with the more fundamental reasons for the growth of British industry. I asked her about the same problem in the interview.

MB: Why was Britain the first to industrialise?
GIRL: I don't know.
MB: What sort of things does a country need before it can industrialise?
GIRL: Money.
MB: Was Britain wealthy in 1750?
GIRL: Yes.
MB: Where had she made this wealth?
GIRL: Trade with the middle East and India.
MB: What evidence is there today that Britain was wealthy in 1750?
GIRL: The houses they built.

Nearly all the pupils showed ignorance of the internally peaceful conditions of Britain in the eighteenth century and her external struggle with France; and nearly all found it hard to equate these conditions in any way with the growth of industry. I asked two boys from Neil if they could think of any ways which wars help industry. They looked at me blankly.

MB: 'Put it another way. Do you think there are any people in America who are glad for financial reasons that war is being fought in Vietnam?

1ST BOY: People that sell guns.

MB: Precisely. Think – that every time a load of bombs is dropped in Vietnam someone . . .

1ST BOY: (*quickly*) . . . is making a profit.'

We went on to discuss the ways in which eighteenth-century wars helped industry. The first boy suggested armour; the second (more accurately) rifles and guns.

MB: 'How does war *hinder* industry?

(*There was no reply.*)

MB: When we were at war with Germany what were the major targets for our bombers?

1ST BOY: Main ports and main manufacturing towns.'

Industrialisation leads logically to the questions on standards of living. These came at the end of the Paper I, Questions 11 & 12 (see p. 174). It was felt that question 11 (i) would be too easy (asking why such a high percentage of the 1825 miner's wages was spent on food), but only thirty-six answers were graded H3 or higher. Several seemed to think that food was the only thing that money could be spent on in those days ('Less things other than food he could spend his money on than today'; 'Not many other things to spend money on'; 'Not other things such as petrol, cinema etc to spend it on'); and many talked about its high cost in 1825. Relative to the miner's wages, of course, food was expensive, but most children who wrote about the price of food gave no indication that they had thought of it in connection with earnings.

The pupils were asked about the problem in the interviews. All of them were clear that the 1825 miner would have earned little, and that today's miner earns £20 or more a week; but nearly all found it remarkably difficult to equate earnings with percentage spent on food. The following conversation is typical of many:

MB: How much do you think a miner earned in 1825?

GIRL: About five shillings a week.

MB: And how much do you think he earns today?

GIRL: Twenty to thirty pounds.

MB: Why do you think the 1825 miner spent such a high proportion of his wages on food?

GIRL: There wasn't so much produced and it was dearer.

MB: Has he a lot of money, the 1825 miner?

GIRL: No.

MB: And what's the most important weekly expenditure he has to make?

GIRL: Food.

MB: Then the reason why he spends such a large proportion of his wage on food is simply because he's . . . (*hoping she will complete my sentence*) . . . got . . . so . . . little.

It may be that the pupils were frightened of stating the obvious; perhaps the percentage put them off; whatever the reason, they nearly all showed an inability to think about the connection between income and expenditure.

The very large proportion of pupils were clear that bread was the most important item of food for the 1825 wage earner – though interestingly the boys of Fairport G S were the group least certain of this, only sixteen out of thirty-three writing 'bread', the remainder putting meat (14) beer and drink (2) or butter (1). It is tempting to infer that this is a reflection of the more affluent class from which the boys come; and certainly their answers to question 11 (ii) (asking for a modern family's three largest recurring items of expenditure over a year, apart from food) give some added support to this view. Fifty-two per cent mentioned cars, petrol or transport, the group coming nearest to this being the boys of Benborough (36 per cent); 61 per cent mentioned pleasure (e.g. cigarettes, drink, entertainment) the boys of Neil coming very near to this with 60 per cent (but only 15 per cent wrote 'car, petrol, transport'). The majority of girls mentioned 'clothes' or 'household' items; gambling was noted four times; one boy wrote gloomily 'bills'. The overall impression is that the pupils are sophisticated enough to appreciate the main items of expenditure in today's world: perhaps they would be clearer about yesterday's standards of living if more time had been spent contrasting and comparing the two situations.

The question asking for two reasons for the fall of bread prices between 1840 and 1895 produced disappointing results, only eight pupils' answers being put in category H. Children of the twentieth century, many were sure that the answer lay in higher production of bread, and answers such as these were very common:

> 'Industrialisation, resulting in increased productivity. Improved communications resulting in faster deliveries of more bread making it cheaper' (boy, B G S).

> 'The use of new machinery meant that bread could be baked more easily. Corn was being produced cheaper by the use of fertilisers which would increase the growth of the corn' (D G S).

> 'Modernisation began to take over therefore it was less expensive to make. As they made more quicker they could sell it for less' (F G S).

> 'Because cheaper methods of making bread were found. Therefore more bread was made so the price went down' (N G S)

> 'Modern machinery produces bread more quickly' (S G S).

Discussion with the pupils soon showed them the limitations of this kind of thinking and forced them to adopt a more logical approach. A girl from Scarcombe had been graded PN2 for this written answer:

> 'This fall in price was due to the fall in cost of production. The workers were still being paid the same wages as . . . [sic]'

I turned her attention to the figures in the interview.

MB: What would be the first question you as an intelligent person would want to ask?

GIRL: Why did it go down rather than up?

MB: (*pointing to the figures*): Is that a big drop?

GIRL: Yes.

MB: What sort of answer would you give?

GIRL: The production became cheaper.

MB: How did you think production costs might have become cheaper?

GIRL: By the use of machinery.

MB: Do you think that's really a plausible theory? . . . Can you give me some example in that fifty-year period of the way in which machinery might have been used in the bread making?

GIRL: The ovens.

MB: Is it really a reasonable theory that mechanisation is introduced during that period to such an extent that the price drops by half?

GIRL: No.

MB: Next point . . .

GIRL: (*pause, then suddenly,*): They were able to get the raw materials cheaper.

MB: What is the basic raw material of bread?

GIRL: Wheat.

MB: Is it a plausible theory that the price of wheat drops substantially during that period?

GIRL: Yes.

MB: Why did the price of wheat drop?

GIRL: They were able to get more of it.

MB: From where?

GIRL: America.

MB: Why were they able to get more of it?

GIRL: Because Britain was trading more with America.

MB: Yes; and in particular what invention – and here you are on machinery – made it possible for large quantities to be brought across swiftly? (*No answer*). What happens if the crossing takes a long time – it's a damp windy crossing?

GIRL: It'll go bad. Well, it will probably begin to sprout.

MB: Have we anything by 1895 that makes this crossing an easier proposition?

GIRL: Steamships.

Here the pupil was forced to think more critically about her first response (virtually a conditioned reply relying on a little ill-digested knowledge about the industrialisation of Britain) and was shown the illogicality of her statement. The right line of thought came as a flash of inspiration once the other unproductive explanations had been explored and discarded.

The following conversation shows another type of thoughtless response being considered more carefully. Two Neil boys had been graded PC3 and PNC3 for their answers to the question on bread prices. In the interviews they thought about the problems again.

1ST BOY: I'd find out who made all the profit on this you know.

MB: I think I'd just do a little bit of hard thinking myself first and begin to put forward a few possible answers; and then we could go and check them up later. Can you, Lewis, think of any possible answer to that fall in price?

106

2ND BOY: Was there more demand – things made in greater quantity?
MB: More demand; it could be . . . . why should there be more demand?
2ND BOY: More people.
MB: And you think that would be enough to account for a fall in price of fifty per cent?
2ND BOY: Not by that amount, no . . .
MB: I think I'd be inclined to push that idea aside.
1ST BOY: The people who made the bread made too much profit in 1840.
MB: That's a possibility. But why should they out of the goodness of their hearts lower the price?
1ST BOY: 'Cos they're forced to 'cos common people have more say in parliament.
MB: By 1895?
1ST BOY: Yes.
MB: Do they?
2ND BOY: No, I think people just couldn't afford to buy it as it was (i.e. the price it was in 1840).
MB: And therefore they had to lower the price?
2ND BOY: Yes.

At this point I asked them what the basic ingredient of bread is, and very quickly they began thinking about wheat. We explored the possibility of greater wheat production in Britain but discarded that as a possible explanation.
MB: You're on the right track: but the price of wheat hasn't gone down because more's being grown in Britain. It is because . . .
1ST BOY: (quickly): . . . more's being grown abroad.
From this point we quickly moved to America, the prairies, combine harvesters and steamships, factors which the boys themselves discovered; I only prompted or queried.

The thoughtlessness shown by many in question 12 (i) was revealed again in the last question of the paper – 'name one group of people who would have been displeased [by this fall in bread prices] and briefly explain why'. A great many pupils automatically (so it seemed) had written 'The bakers, because they would make less profit'; once again the interview could make them face their illogicality.
MB: Who's going to dislike this fall in prices? [We had been discussing the figures and had thought about the importation of cheap corn from abroad.]
GIRL: The rich farmers. They can't produce wheat at such low prices. [She had put in her test paper: 'Merchants selling other goods which would have been bought in place of bread'.]
MB: Therefore the person who suffers is the farmer – Oh (to catch her out) and the baker; he's selling his bread for fivepence instead of tenpence.
GIRL: Yes, he can't make such a profit.
MB: Is that really true? Who determines the price of bread?
GIRL: There must be some fixed price, I suppose.

MB: I wouldn't say so. I'd say it's the manufacturer. And who is the manufacturer?

GIRL: The baker.

MB: And what determines his actual price?

GIRL: What he pays for the actual flour.

MB: And has that gone down in price?

GIRL: Yes.

MB: Therefore his profit has not gone down . . .

Standards of living and world affairs have a close connection for Britain today; and four questions were set in the history tests to probe the pupils' awareness of other countries. Question 7, paper I, is concerned with the times of industrialisation of countries other than Britain, questions 9 and 10, paper I, with population problems, section three, paper II, with world civilisations. Of the four questions, number 10 (victories of small populations over larger) was least satisfactory both statistically and semantically; the question oversimplifies situations which in practice were extremely complex, and the pupils' answers reflected this lack of precision. The rest were more successful; in conjunction with the interviews they revealed astonishing areas of ignorance, particularly about the two giants of the world, China and Russia.

The pupils' scores on question 7 (which allows little scope for error) were surprisingly low (see p. 173 for the question, p. 182 for the marking scheme). Only 43 per cent were able to score 9 out of 10 or full marks; and nearly a third of the children were unable to recognise Communist China as the most recent of the group to industrialise.

How accurately do the scores represent the pupils' knowledge? In the interviews the matter was probed more fully. It was found that in every school enough pupils revealed uncertainty or ignorance of this crucial aspect of world development for the orientation of the syllabus to be questioned.

A boy from Benborough, for example, considered that the United States started her industrialisation in 1800 and that she gained independence from Britain in 1856 (his order was Britain, U S A, Russia, France); a Fairport boy made a similar remark. A girl from D G S (who scored 10 in the test) showed uncertainty in the interview.

MB: Did Russia fight in the second world war?

GIRL: Um . . . Yes.

MB: What were the dates of the war?

GIRL: (*with no hesitation*): 1939 to 1945.

MB: Did Russia have any industry then?

GIRL: Not as much as Germany.

MB: Did she make weapons, machinery?

GIRL: I don't think so.

MB: What about China.

GIRL: I don't think so.

Often the pupils would show that their first answers were little more than random guesses. A Daymer girl, for example, had put Russia immediately after Britain on the ladder but in the interview said that Russia had no industry in 1939; an N G S boy whose order in the test was Britain, France, Germany, Communist China, India, United States, said he would put China or Russia last; a Scarcombe girl thought that Communist China began to industrialise about 1900, Russia about 1920 (her test order was Britain, United States, France, India, Germany); a boy from Neil, that Russia started industrialisation in 1800, Communist China in 1850, France in 1900 and Germany most recently (test order: Britain, United States, Germany, India, France).

Such answers, of course, stem from ignorance of the facts; yet this ignorance is of a more fundamental nature than, say, not knowing the date of the battle of Waterloo. The latter is a discrete piece of information, the former concerned with the structure and pattern of society; and ignorance of this shows a failure to recognise relationships and developments which give meaning and shape to so much of nineteenth-century history. But it seemed that most of the pupils were being confronted with a problem which they had never met before, and a Daymer girl's remark was typical of this attitude.

GIRL: I was a bit sort of shocked to see it really. I didn't expect to see it.
MB: Is it important do you think?
GIRL: Yes, I think so – the relationship of our country to others. It seems jolly interesting.

Question 9 looks at populations in Britain and other countries. The problem was something new for the pupils, too, and a Fairport boy remarked:

'I didn't really like it – it seemed pointless, quite honestly. Well, I suppose if I'd known how to answer it, it would have been more sensible to me. But I didn't know how to answer it because we haven't touched on anything like it before.'

The answers revealed uncertainty for though many were able to write and talk about a high death rate and low standard of living in nineteenth-century China and the immigration to the United States, their understanding of the problems tended to remain at a high level of generality. In particular, there was less ignorance about nineteenth-century immigration to America and many could only think in terms of the seventeenth-century and eighteenth-century settlers, reflecting syllabuses that deal with the early colonial period but say little about the European exodus of the nineteenth century. Of course, it is true that the figures may have put some off the question (there is no evidence here to suggest that the girls were at a disadvantage); and one boy (the only pupil to do so) showed up a flaw in the rubric by writing in answer to question 9 (ii) ('Why do you think the U S A's population increase is so very much greater than those of the other three?')

'It didn't. China had the most increase. It is just that there was a low figure in 1800. The rise was only 177 million, China was 500 million.'

In the interview, however, he was prompted to think about the proportional increase. We had been talking about immigration to America.

MB: Where do you think the people came from?

BOY: Well, I suppose from the figures from China. They could be going from China to the U.S.A., though it's very doubtful.

MB: Do you think this was the nineteenth century?

BOY: Not in the nineteenth century.

MB: When?

BOY: Well, quite all the time. They've been sort of flowing over there all the time through the years.

This reply (and to a certain extent his written answer) reveals a way of thinking that was shown by many of the pupils. The children found it difficult to reason outside the framework of the material they had been given. Presented with figures on population increase many thought the answer lay in the numbers alone; given the passages to comment on the majority only used the material in front of them. Often the opposite was true as well. For example, in many of the interviews when talking about population I would start by describing the relatively slow increase of world population up to about 1750, often drawing a sketch graph. I would contrast this with the population explosion of the late eighteenth and nineteenth centuries. 'Why did population increase so slowly up to 1750?', I would ask, sometimes adding, 'Smaller families perhaps?' Most pupils quickly mentioned a high death rate; and I was able to transfer their attention to nineteenth-century China. Did they think she would have a high death rate in the nineteenth century? Yes, nearly all of them did think so, mentioning a low standard of living, poor medical facilities, and so on. Yet when they were asked to look again at the figures and explain the reason for the low proportional increase in China's population, few were able to transfer the knowledge they had already displayed to the tabular situation. It is only possible to speculate on the reasons for this: it may be partly the fear of venturing outside a known territory; it may be a reflection of the teaching methods which in their efforts to cover the ground make too few demands on imaginative effort.[1]

Section three, paper II (p. 177), looks at Europe and the wider world. The section is based on a Pacific orientated map of the world on which are marked seven social and cultural groups or spheres of influence existing in 1450: Europe, Islam, India, China, Japan and the empires of the Aztecs and Incas.

The inadequacies of the section should be pointed out at the start: the rubric was perhaps a little complicated ('social and cultural spheres of influence' is rather ponderous and difficult for fifteen-year-olds; the phrase was used to avoid the word 'civilisation' with its Toynbeean overtones),

[1] Similar points are discussed by John Holt in his book *Why Children Fail*, Pitman, 1964. Though dealing principally with the teaching of mathematics, his aim is to show how a child's potential for learning is often stifled by the framework and pressures of the classroom.

and the phrase 'dealt with' in question (*b*) may have been too limiting. One girl showed a splendidly legal mind when she explained in the interview why she did not attempt the question.

'I didn't do it because I hadn't learned anything . . . I couldn't answer the question. It says "Name three Europeans (explorers, scientists)". Well, I could have done that part; and then it says "who were responsible for extending European knowledge of one or more of these areas". But I don't exactly know how they were responsible for extending European knowledge because Christopher Columbus sailed and he discovered – well, I forget what he discovered – West Indies or something. Nobody knew where they were so he couldn't have been extending knowledge.'

Even so the section was valuable and showed the limitations of the pupils' thought in this sphere. In question (*a*) the great majority mentioned the great explorers, and the names 'Marco Polo', 'Columbus', 'Vasco da Gama', 'Magellan' came up with regularity. One or two tried to be a little more adventurous but as a result often strayed outside the terms of the question; for example, the seven pupils who mentioned Captain Cook or the four who wrote 'Livingstone'. Nine, however, put 'Clive', one 'Dalhousie', another with some ingenuity 'Samuel Morse and Henry Ford'. A Daymer girl wrote, 'Napoleon, Drake, Columbus. Drake and Columbus just discovered other countries. Napoleon went round the world and brought ideas to France – e.g. culture'; she was, perhaps, dimly remembering a lesson on the Egyptian expedition. For the most part, however, the answers were tied to the early days of discovery and with the exception of the girl who noted 'Ford and Morse' none thought of the transport and communication revolutions and the great names connected with these.

The Europeans' treatment of the seven areas was asked about in question (*b*). Reference here was mainly to the Aztecs and Incas and to India. Most of those who mentioned the two American civilisations wrote in terms of the Spaniards' cruelty:

'The inhabitants were badly treated by Cortez and many died because they were made to do hard labour' (D G S).

'The Spaniards overran the Inca civilisation and destroyed their beautiful work and looted their jewels and gold' (F G S).

'The Spanish treated them exceedingly badly often wiping them out and destroying the towns, ravaging for gold and taking it' (N G S).

Several pupils showed no understanding of European contacts with these civilisations. Three clearly had never heard or seen the words before, writing 'Azteo' and 'Inoa' (the 'c' on the duplicated map was not very clear). Others wrote in this vein:

'The Europeans brought gifts to pacify the Incas to win their friendship' (boy, B G S).

'The settlers didn't use force or bloodshed to gain the country. They negotiated and paid for the land they settled in' (D G S).

111

'On very good terms with each other' (s G s).

'Made peace with them and have understandings with them' (s G s).

Fifty-seven mentioned India and for the most part emphasised the colonisation and subjection of the Indians and the exploitation of their wealth. Fourteen of these pupils, however, tried to paint a more favourable picture. For example:

'In India the British dealt fairly friendly and spread the Western ideas around but unfortunately this was not appreciated at first' (boy, B G s).

'India was reasonably well looked after and was guided on the way to becoming a civilised country' (F G s).

'After 1450 Europeans helped the inhabitants in ways of life taught them religion and taught them ways of civilised life' (N G s).

Civilisation is equated with Western Europe, and the Benborough boy's comment above shows signs of the surprise the Victorians used to feel when English culture was rejected. An F G s boy revealed a touching faith in the stability of British Imperialism when he wrote: 'The Indians were formed into states. If any "riots" were started there was always an English army to intervene'.

China was noted by only ten pupils, five of whom were from Scarcombe, two from Neil, one from Fairport and two from Benborough; Islam by eight pupils, six of whom were from Fairport; and Japan by four pupils. The quality of answers here was very poor and the pupils clearly had little knowledge. The pupils of Benborough merely wrote that the Europeans traded with the Chinese; a Fairport boy noted vaguely that 'they were left mainly to themselves', adding as an afterthought 'except for a few explorers'; a boy from Neil and a girl from Scarcombe talked about Marco Polo, crediting him with the establishment of friendly relations between the two civilisations and the spread of European languages in China. The only thoughtful comment came from a Scarcombe pupil who wrote 'The Europeans moved in but could not take over, instead they made little "town" colonies separate from each other.'

The eight who mentioned Islam wrote almost exclusively in terms of the crusades and religion (a Scarcombe girl noted briefly 'The Europeans took slaves from Islam'); and those who wrote about Japan were succinct.

'A small amount of trading done' (F G s).

'Traded for spices etc.' (N G s).

'Fought in the second world war' (s G s).

'Europe fought with Japan in the second world war' (s G s).

It would seem therefore that many of these pupils' knowledge of the outside world is brief and fragmented; and I would surmise that this is true of the majority of secondary school children. Those who believe that a world orientated syllabus must replace the traditional course will consider that the demands for contemporary and world history made by the pupils in chapter 2 and the attitude of the senior history teachers are given added urgency by the results of the tests.

The houses illustrated in section 4, paper II (p. 177) and the four sections of paper III (p. 178) looked for responses of a slightly different calibre than the answers already discussed. It has been shown these rely more directly on factual knowledge; though in each case understanding of the structural implications of the facts was looked for rather than the discrete pieces of information. But a pupil who had, for example, just spent three periods on the repeal of the corn laws would presumably have been able to answer the question on bread prices more effectively than one who had never heard of the events of 1846. On the other hand, the photographs and extracts in the remaining sections asked the pupils to range more widely over the history they had covered, and the quality of their answers was less dependent on the specific topics they had been taught than on the broad understandings the history teaching had awakened in them.

It was perhaps because of this that the photographs of houses roused such opposition from some pupils: there was a feeling that such matters 'weren't history'.

1ST GIRL: (S G s) 'I don't think it's got much to do with history.

2ND GIRL: Well, history really is concerned with facts and dates isn't it?

MB: It's not concerned with ideas?

2ND GIRL: No, not much.'

A Fairport boy thought it was 'rather an odd question really' and another commented: 'It's not a bad idea but it's not really relevant to history as we understand it.' 'As we understand it': the words, so casually uttered, convey the limitations and restrictions of a history course which not only concentrates on the rote learning of information rather than the exploration of ideas but also tends to emphasise the political, constitutional and economic aspects of history at the expense of the social, cultural and artistic. Indeed, there is a tendency amongst teachers and pupils to consider that these latter three hold a lower status than the former; and when, for example, a lesson or two is grudgingly given on architecture or a similar subject, the treatment is often more superficial than that accorded to the traditional topics. Certainly the pupils' written answers to the questions on the photographs of houses often showed little flexibility or imagination. Take, for example, the following extracts from answers to the first question which asked for a comparison and explanation of the building methods used in the construction of the half-timbered and the modern semi-detached houses.

'The windows in A have bars across them' (girl B G s).

'In A the upper storey leans out, in C it does not because in the sixteenth century they often had shops under the houses on the lower floor' (D G s).

'You could get more houses in a road by terracing but didn't need in 1940' s (sic)' (F G s).

'The houses in C have gardens unlike those in A' (N G S).

'In C the houses are more spaced out. We have more houses now and don't need to crush them all together' (S G S).

These answers show two characteristics which occurred frequently. Many pupils seized on an obvious point ('the houses in C have gardens'; 'they have bigger windows'; 'they are uniform') but would be unable to give any explanation of the contrast: others, on the other hand, would advance an explanation that was hardly rational ('The upper storey leans out because they had shops under';' . . . it is easier to clean larger panes of glass than small ones' (a girl); 'houses today are built to live in and are not for decoration').

The comparison of living conditions in the eighteenth century with the twentieth century (photographs B and C) provoked inummerable comments on the squalor and monotony of rural cottage life; and indeed, the picture of the contented rustic of the eighteenth century as yet uncontaminated by the industrial revolution is one that bears little resemblance to the real situation. But the pupils showed a certain smug acceptance of suburban life with its 'mod. cons.' and bustling social life – attitudes echoed in answers to question (c) which asked for a comparison between sixteenth-century Mill Street and the twentieth-century ribbon development. Here are five typical comments on the quality of life in the sixteenth century.

'They would not have much privacy because the houses were built against each other. The risk of fire or disease spreading would be much greater' (girl, B G S).

'They got on each others nerves. It would be a good place for vermin and that would be bound to effect them' (D G S).

'Very unhealthy – disease would spread quickly, washing clothes would be difficult' (F G S).

'If fire broke out it would spread easily. Made the place hard to clean' (N G S).

'Fire and disease could be easily spread. No room for grass verges or trees' (S G S).

This is what the same pupils had to say about the twentieth-century housing of photograph B.

'They could have bigger gardens and it would be much better for health. They would have a much wider view' (girl, B G S).

'They probably didn't like the houses because they are like everybody elses. There is better sanitation' (D G S).

'Often transport was hard to come by. Houses were shably built because the builders were in such a hurry' (F G S).

'Makes easy access to the main road to go to work or school etc. Lets more light get at the houses, so as to make them look fresher' (N G S).

114

'Living in a ribbon development would make it difficult to really get into the country. Communications with the actual town might be bad' (s G s).

These latter remarks do not give unqualified approval to the monotonous string of houses; but to all of this group, a life in the sprawl of the twentieth-century housing would seem preferable to one in the tightly knit community of Mill Street. Such an attitude is understandable; the pupils can hardly be blamed for preferring the technological advances and comforts of their own age. What the answers to these questions showed clearly, however, was the way the pupils concentrated on the tangible aspects of sixteenth-century and twentieth-century living conditions and have failed to write about the quality of structure of life. Thus fire, dirt, disease, lack of privacy are mentioned time and again in connection with Mill Street; gardens, public services, danger from the roads with the ribbon development; but very few have made the imaginative effort to consider the photographs in the context of the two different periods and so perhaps grasp the sense of place, identity and belonging which characterises the sixteenth-century community (basically static) in contrast with today's restless society, which is always hurrying on its way.

Stonehenge standing massive and powerful on the flat expanse of Salisbury plain; the temple of Isis brooding darkly; Lincoln cathedral's nave holding the vault of heaven in its grasp: how do the pupils react to the photographs of these powerful pieces of architecture which form the basis of paper III's first section? The answers were disappointing; in question (a) ('What distinctive impression does each building convey to you?') only one person was graded H: in (b) ('What differences in man's idea of God can you see in the three religious buildings?'), six. This Neil boy's answer to the first question was the only one to merit an H3 grading.

> *Stonehenge:* Originally had a plan with all the building contained in a circle, gives the impression of some sort of ancient temple for sacrificing.

> *Temple of Isis:* Looks very mysterious and secret giving the impression of a private prayer house which one has to take great pains to enter.

> *Lincoln Cathedral:* Looks very architectural indeed as it is a house far superior than any other, giving the impression that the church was at its greatest power then.

Contrast this with the following answer from a Scarcombe girl graded PN2.

> 1. The π-shaped stones are right in the centre of an incomplete ring of pillars.
> 2. The drawings of people are quite lifelike.
> 3. The design of the interior of the cathedral is all symmetrical.

Though the boy is rather clumsy in his writing, he is straining to express his reactions to the photographs and to make an imaginative effort. He senses the stark cruelty of Stonehenge and the secretive, fearful atmosphere of the Egyptian temple (which he tries to convey in the words ' . . . private prayer house . . . one has to take great pains to enter'); he is sensitive to the delicate majesty of Lincoln cathedral. The girl has done little more than detach and note the external features of the buildings – the shape of the stones, the drawings of the people, the design of the interior; she has made no attempt to think imaginatively about these photographs and to evaluate them as a whole. This was the hallmark of the very great majority of answers to both parts of the section, and the one or two answers which transcended the immediate content of the photographs stood out markedly from the rest. The only two H1 responses to question (b) must be quoted here for they are outstanding examples of the sort of sensitivity that children can achieve. The first is from Gardiner of Fairport. It has been noted that his I Q is only 114 – (see p. 99); the second is from a Daymer girl whose I Q of 144 is the highest of the sample.

'In the first, God seems to be a vague, malevolent spirit who must be placated by sacrifice. In the second, he or they are a set of omnipotent beings with human failings, and in the third he appears as a divine, all seeing God from far above. The last point is marked out by the soaring pillars and roof of the Cathedral.'

'In the first photograph, man's idea of God was as rough and crude as the stones that made Stonehenge. They thought he was vengeful and cruel. In the second photograph, the Egyptians thought also that God was vengeful, but somewhere beauty got into their idea of God. In the last photograph man's idea of God is that of forgiveness and grace and magnitude.'

In both these there is a control of language and economy of words which I find admirable. Though the comments are based directly on the photographs, they draw on knowledge already in the pupil's possession; the children's thinking has been used to shape and interpret these historical data with a fine degree of understanding.

Such mental flexibility and daring was shown all too rarely; and in the following two sections (a verse from the Song of Roland contrasted with 'Dulce et Decorum est', and a comparison between extracts from two accounts of visits to sixteenth- and nineteenth-century London) only twenty responses (ten in section two, ten in section three) were put in category H1, none in subcategory H1. Most of the answers were firmly tied to the given material; like the comments on the photographs in the previous section and in paper II, the pupil clung to the 'facts' before them.

Limited time, however, may have affected the quality of answers in these two sections for they are the longest in the batch of tests. In each there is a considerable amount of reading to be done; and though it did not seem during the investigation of the test that the pupils were rushed, one or two referred to the time factor in the interviews. A Daymer girl,

for example, was graded PN1 for her answer to section two (see page 178).
I asked her if she liked the question.

GIRL: Yes, I like poetry . . .

MB: Does the fact that they lived at different times explain the difference between them?

GIRL: Yes, I think it does. I suppose one could say that in the ninth century it was considered the thing to fight to gain power and position; and nowadays it's a thing people avoid.

MB: Why?

GIRL: Because it causes so much after affects.

MB: Worse than the ninth century?

GIRL: Yes – the weapons are so much more advanced – they seem to affect the whole being nowadays.

MB: Why didn't you say that in the exam?

GIRL: Well, I think perhaps I read it through and being pressed for time I didn't really think.

Yet the limitations of thought here (and elsewhere in the test papers) stemmed mainly from mental inertness rather than the time limitations; when the pupils were directly confronted with the questions and made to press home a thought process they could show a greater flexibility. A Fairport boy, for example, was graded PC3 for this response:

'Roland only thinks of the war as a way of gaining honours. He does not think of his soldiers. The other poet voices the soldiers' feelings as they are marched from point to point under gas attack, so tired they cannot even hear or see. This poet shows war to be a way of killing men which solves nothing.'

Here his thinking is tied very closely to the content of the poems, even to the extent of repeating their words. I asked him in the interviews to think again about the poems and see if he could explain the difference.

BOY: 'Well for Roland it was more of a personal affair. You went up to someone, you had a hand to hand fight with your sword; but in this one you were 500 yards away . . . it was completely impersonal.

MB: What did society think about war in the first one?

BOY: In the first one they thought it was a great adventure and were very proud of their people going out fighting. In the second one they were proud of them but they didn't think it was a great adventure.'

This discussion shows him beginning to venture outside the bounds of the material: the question which starts him speculating, and prompts him to take the imaginative leap forward, is the query about society's attitude.

But the question had to be posed by the teacher; few pupils seem able to extend their thinking by asking themselves questions. A girl from B G S referred to this after we had been discussing the effects of the Industrial revolution in London.

'Well you don't think of that when you're doing this sort of thing [i.e. comparing the two extracts of section three]. You first look at the two

117

paragraphs and compare them but you don't think of any other aspect of history. You're just dealing with that at the time it's written.'

The answers of two Benborough girls to section three are typical examples of responses that 'just deal with the extracts at the time they were written': they were graded PC2 and PC3.

MB: Can you explain the differences [between the two extracts] to me?

1ST GIRL: Well, in that one it's all wealthy. In that one it's all poor.

MB: You're just pointing out a difference to me: you're not explaining it.

1ST GIRL: Well, it shows that in the earlier time there wasn't so much poverty.

MB: What caused this change?

2ND GIRL: It shows the effect of the revolution on London.

MB: Which revolution?

2ND GIRL: The industrial revolution.

MB: What is the attitude of the second writer to the poverty he sees? Is it indifference, contempt – or is he disturbed about it?

2ND GIRL: I think he's more disturbed by it.

MB: What particular sentence or phrase would you point out?

2ND GIRL: I think the last sentence when he mentions that some families have no bed other than a heap of soot.

MB: Look at the first extract, the second and fourth paragraphs. Can you point out something he mentions which would shock us today?

1ST GIRL: The way you've got the heads stuck on spikes.

MB: What shows he isn't very shocked?

1ST GIRL: Well, he's just carried on explaining it.

MB: And in the fourth paragraph?

1ST GIRL: Baiting of bulls and bears.

MB: Why do you think there is this indifference in the first writer compared with the compassion of the second? Is it just that the German is indifferent to suffering?

2ND GIRL: Well, in the first one people were used to that – everyone went to the bull baiting and things like that.

MB: Why the change?

2ND GIRL: Because the general standard of living has risen for most people.

MB: And not for others?

2ND GIRL: Well, some people don't seem to have kept up with the change.

MB: Good point. Can you think of a movement today which has made ordinary people aware of poverty and suffering?

2ND GIRL (*quickly*): Oxfam.

MB: Were there movements like this in the nineteenth century, making ordinary people much more conscious of what's going on?

2ND GIRL: Yes.

Two boys from the same school were prompted in their interview to take the point of growing social awareness a stage further. The first boy gained a PNC2 for his written response, the second PC3.

118

MB: Can you mention two things in the first extract that we today would find horrifying?

1ST BOY: The heads of those executed. Baiting of bulls and bears.

MB: Does he disapprove?

2ND BOY: No, he thought it was great fun, apparently.

MB: What about the attitude of the second writer? Is he indifferent – or is he trying to excite our sympathy?

1ST BOY: I'd say he was trying to excite our sympathy.

MB: Can we explain this contrast in historical terms too? Have people become more socially conscious by the nineteenth century?

2ND BOY: Yes, because . . . they've introduced a no hanging bill quite recently.

MB: But that's 1965.

2ND BOY: Yes, but it has progressed right up to that, hasn't it really?

MB: Can you think of any acts of parliament of the nineteenth century in this context?

1ST BOY: The Whig acts of the 1830's.

MB: Can you give me some examples?

1ST BOY: Poor Law Amendment Act.

2ND BOY: National Insurance.

MB: Ah – but when's that?

2ND BOY: That's the twentieth-century.

MB: Can you think of any groups of people who made people aware of social evil?

1ST BOY: Later, the Fabian society.

MB: A very good one.

2ND BOY: The Chartists: the anti-corn-law league.

MB: Any individual people?

2ND BOY: William Wilberforce.

1ST BOY: Lord Shaftesbury.

MB: Any women?

1ST BOY: Florence Nightingale.

MB: Can you think of a modern movement which has done a great deal to arouse public conscience about poverty and starvation abroad?

1ST BOY: Oxfam.

In both these cases the questions led the pupils on, and they were put in positions where they were forced to delve deeply and draw on the discrete pieces of information they had at their disposal. They were, in fact, beginning to structure their knowledge and present it in coherent form.

CONCLUDING REMARKS

The above paragraphs have shown that on the whole the pupils revealed more flexibility of thought in the interviews than in the tests; that when pressed to consider a question they could often show an ability to diverge and think outside the confines of the material, drawing on information they had acquired. In short, many showed that they had the capacity for structuring their knowledge into meaningful form through the interaction of thought and fact. However, many pupils seemed surprised that history could involve such mental activity.

'We had to think more because in the other history exam [school exam] you just put down the facts; but in these you had to know just more than facts. You had to think a bit' (boy, B G S).

'They're interesting because it shows what you've taken in. . . . What we do is the sort of top layer of history – that [the research tests] goes right down underneath, you say what you think underneath it's about. See what I mean?' (B G S).

'They were something new – quite interesting. You put your mind to it and try and work out the answers. . . . We haven't been used to doing that sort of work' (F G S).

'We get fed up with the normal routine . . . With this it made us think more about what we were doing, what we had done in history' (N G S).
And from the same school a short conversation which exemplifies G. H. Bantock's remarks that grammar school efficiency enables pupils to accumulate data but that the syllabus is rarely thought of as a means of revelation: [1]

BOY: I preferred them to an examination. You don't have to spend time on revision beforehand – and you use your imagination more. You don't have to be clever. You have to think.

MB: Do you have to think in history normally?

BOY: Well, most subjects now it's copying out of the book – reading and writing it.

MB: Most subjects? Do you find, for example, that's the way geography's taught?

BOY: Yes – copying notes and maps.

MB: Is that the way English is taught?

BOY: That's one subject where you're taught and you just have to do exercises.

Finally, from Scarcombe grammar school: 'I think that [the research tests] was testing your real knowledge. I mean when you go in for an exam, you learn what you have to learn and nothing more.'

Such remarks may only indicate the pupil's desire to please; but the same children could be blunt enough in other circumstances. The pupils did seem to feel that the tests and interviews were asking them to think relevantly and meaningfully – that they were probing 'real knowledge'; whereas much of school history seems remote, disjointed and unreal – or as one girl said, 'You learn the facts but they don't seem relative to us'.

The interviews showed clearly that secondary school pupils have the ability to structure and use their knowledge, and to think in a way which can make the subject vital and relevant. Often, however, history teaching

[1] G. H. Bantock, *Education in an Industrial Society*, Faber, 1963, p. 172.

makes too few demands on the intellect. By the fourth or fifth year, lessons become geared to the external examination, and the pupils' history learning takes the form of unthinking receptivity rather than independent activity. Teachers ensure that the children are well rehearsed and can repeat accurately the information the questions demand; and the pressures these examinations are felt to exert seem to allow little or no time for more worthwhile activities in history. The pupils who took part in this investigation generally answered the history test papers in the mechanical, unthinking way such teaching produces and it was only when challenged and confronted with the problems in the interviews that they began to show more flexibility.

Reshaping the purpose and form of the present external history examinations will not, of course, solve the problems of history classroom practice. But the construction of examinations similar to the ones used in this investigation could set an example of thoughtful history teaching and promote a situation in which challenge and response take over from one-sided instruction and rote learning.

6 Conclusion

The problems of history syllabus content, teaching technique and assessment which this book has explored are in need of urgent discussion; and it is hoped that the survey of the five curricula and the recommendations which are made will contribute to the debate and suggest new ways of meeting the opportunities of secondary school history. So far as the syllabus is concerned, the results of the investigation strengthen the argument that we must abandon the English history outlines approach and replace it with a course based on world orientated themes which culminate in the fourth and fifth years in a study of twentieth-century history. More than this, the syllabus must no longer deal principally with constitutional, diplomatic or political history; and there is a strong case for closer cooperation with, say, the English, geography and religious education departments so that history becomes a house in which many subjects meet. A number of schools have had success with team teaching; and parts of the syllabus given in this book are well suited to this approach.

Perhaps the point which emerges most clearly from the investigation is that teaching methods need as much consideration as teaching content. We may have exciting syllabuses dealing with recent and world history; we may issue the glossiest and latest of textbooks; but all this can achieve no more than the most reactionary of courses if the methods used fail to illuminate. We are still wedded to techniques which tend to deaden rather than inspire; and so long as we believe that pupils must be told rather than discover for themselves there is little possibility of uncovering their potential for creative, divergent thought.

But the winds of change are blowing through the secondary schools, winds which are ruffling even the placid backwaters of traditional history teaching. The C S E encourages teachers to take direct control of their fourth and fifth year courses; curriculum research is devising new syllabuses and new techniques of examining: in every subject the traditional patterns of teaching are being challenged. Such challenges might prompt the redrafting of English outline syllabuses, the loosening of authoritarian teaching techniques and the construction by teachers and examination boards of valid and reliable tests which take greater account of historical thinking, less of the mere repetition of facts. These might be ways of making history a relevant and vital subject for today's children – a means of enabling every pupil to echo the words of one boy who wrote:
    'Learning history is very beneficial. I find history an extremely good subject to have a conversation on, and I think that to know facts, such

as historical facts, gives you a broader outlook on life. It builds your character because it gives you boldness of speech! '

and then finally, in capital letters,

'I THOROUGHLY ENJOY HISTORY.'

Bibliography

This bibliography lists some of the important and relevant works of interest to history teachers. Books for use with pupils are given at the end of the chapter on the syllabus (pp. 32 to 52). Books on local history are listed on page 81.

1. Teaching of history

Mention should first be made of the Historical Association whose wide range of activities and publications (including the magazine *History*) are of particular value to the teacher. Especially useful are its 'Aids for Teachers' series and 'Teaching of History' leaflets. As well as the school textbook library (mentioned on p. 32), the Association has a well stocked history library at its headquarters in London; and for both these collections catalogues are issued. There are branches of the Historical Association throughout the country, and these organise lectures and other meetings. To join the H A or to obtain further details of its work, aims and services to teachers, write to the Hon. Secretary, The Historical Association, 59a Kennington Park Road, London, S E 11.

The *Handbook for History Teachers* (ed. W. H. Burston and C. W. Green Methuen, 1962) warrants particular mention too. This covers virtually every aspect of history teaching. It has comprehensive bibliographies of history books for every age group, including the sixth form; it lists and comments on visual aids; it has articles on the teaching of history. It is, in short, an invaluable book.

Other important publications are:

W. H. BURSTON, *Principles of History Teaching*, Methuen, 1963

P. CARPENTER, *History Teaching: the era approach*, Cambridge University Press, 1964

DEPARTMENT OF EDUCATION AND SCIENCE, *Towards World History*, Education pamphlet No. 52, H M S O, London, 1967

SHEILA FERGUSON, *Projects in History*, Batsford, 1967

F. C. HAPPOLD, *The Approach to History*, Christophers, London, 1928

I. A. A. M., *The Teaching of History in Secondary Schools*, Cambridge University Press, third edition, 1965

M. V. C. JEFFREYS, *History in Schools: the study of development*, Pitman, 1948

E. M. LEWIS, *Teaching History in Secondary Schools*, Evans, 1960

E. AND E. K. MILLIKEN, *Handwork Methods in the Teaching of History*, Wheaton, 1949

SCHOOLS COUNCIL, *The Certificate of Secondary Education: the place of the personal topic: History*, Examinations Bulletin No. 18, H M S O, London, 1968

C. F. STRONG, *History in the Secondary School*, University of London Press, 1958

Other relevant books

B.S. BLOOM et al. (editors),*Taxonomy of Educational Objectives, Handbook 1: The Cognitive Domain; Handbook 2: The Affective Domain.* English editions, Longmans, 1965

J. HOLT, *How Children Fail*, Pitman, 1964

L. HUDSON, *Contrary Imaginations: a psychological study of the English school boy*, Methuen, 1966

D. R. MATHER, N. FRANCE AND G. T. SARE, *The Certificate of Secondary Education: a handbook for moderators*, Collins, 1965

SCHOOLS COUNCIL, *The Certificate of Secondary Education: some suggestions for examiners*, Examinations Bulletin No. 1, H M S O, London, 1963

2. Research publications

Details of researches into the problems of history teaching and learning presented for higher degrees in the universities in the United Kingdom and Ireland can be found in Blackwell's lists which go back to 1918.

A. M. BLACKWELL, *Lists of Researches in Education and Educational Psychology*, published for the National Foundation for Educational Research in England and Wales by Newnes Educational Publishing Co. Ltd.

Blackwell's final list (supplement III) deals with the years 1956-57; but the National Foundation for Educational Research produces occasional publications which give details of current research projects. The registers go back to 1959.

National Foundation for Educational Research in England and Wales, *Current Researches in Education and Educational Psychology*, N F E R.

All theses accepted for higher degrees are listed in the Aslib Index which is published annually and goes back to 1950.

P. D. RECORD, ed., *Index of Theses Accepted for Higher Degrees in the Universities of Great Britain and Ireland*, Association of Special Libraries and Information Bureaux.

3. Articles

Published articles in British periodicals on the teaching and learning of history are catalogued in the British Education Index. The index goes back to 1954; it is now published three times a year.

The Librarians of Institutes of Education, comp. *British Education Index*, Library Association.

Details of other articles on history can be found in the British Humanities Index. In 1962 this index superseded the Subject Index to Periodicals which was first published in 1915 and was issued annually except for the years 1923–25. Since 1954 it has been published quarterly.

PETER FERRIDAY, ed.. *British Humanities Index*, Library Association.

Appendix I

Teachers' questionnaire

1. Name of school? ....
2. Year of foundation? ....
3. Age of entry? ....
4. Method of selection? ....
5. Size of school? ....
6. Average size of classes in the lower school? ....
7. 'O' level examination board for history? ....
8. Average number of candidates entered for history 'O' level in the last three years? ....
9. Number of pupils doing history for 'A' and 'S' level in
   a. 1st year VI ....
   b. 2nd year VI ....
   c. 3rd year VI ....
10. Does the school 'stream' pupils
    a. on the basis of the entry examination results.
    b. at the end of the FIRST/SECOND year.
    c. at some later stage in the school.
    d. The school does not stream pupils.
    Please underline the appropriate statement.
11. How many forms cover the 'O' level course in four years? ....
12. a. Does the school 'set' pupils for history in the lower school? YES/NO
    b. If YES, please indicate in what year(s) this is done ....
13. a. Does history become an optional subject at any stage in the lower school? YES/NO.
    b. If YES, please indicate when the subject becomes optional ......
14. Please complete the following table:

Specialist History teachers	Years of experience	Years in present post	Teaching certificate
Head of department			
1			
2			
3			

15. Total number of periods in each week/cycle? ....
16. Please complete the following table, bracketing where possible:

Year	Form/set	Number of History periods per week	Taught History by	Number of History homeworks per week	Time to be spent on homework	School examinations term(s) held
1	....	....	....	....	....	
	....	....	....	....	....	
	....	....	....	....	....	
2	....	....	....	....	....	
	....	....	....	....	....	
	....	....	....	....	....	
3	....	....	....	....	....	
	....	....	....	....	....	
	....	....	....	....	....	
4	....	....	....	....	....	
	....	....	....	....	....	
	....	....	....	....	....	

17. How much money is available for:

    a. Text books ....   *d.* Equipment ....

    b. Library books ....   *e.* Excursions ....

    c. Maps ....

    If sum is not constant, give approximate annual average.

18. Please underline the items of equipment available: add others not included.

    Episcope   Television

    Filmstrip projector   Tape recorder

    Film projector (sound/silent)   Gramophone

    Radio   Duplicator

19. Please indicate in the table below the availability (e.g. Yes: no: can borrow) and quantity (e.g. Numerous: a small collection) of the following items. Please add any material you use not included in the list.

Material	Availability	Quantity
Wall maps		
Slides		
Filmstrips		
Films		
Reproductions of historical material (e.g. Jackdaw series)		
Local material		

20. Please indicate below any *sets* of historical books available for class or homework in the lower school (e.g. Then and There series).
21. Are all pupils issued with an atlas? YES/NO
22. Is the history library in the MAIN SCHOOL LIBRARY/HISTORY ROOM?
23. Do pupils in the lower school (i.e. up to and including 'O' level forms) have access to these books? YES/NO

24. *The History Room.* Please complete the following tables by ticking in the appropriate columns.

a. The room.

	Good	Adequate	Poor	Additional comments
Size				
Shape				
Desks/chairs				
Blackboard				
Blackout				
Display boards				
Library space				
Storage space				

b. Teaching in the History Room

Year	Periods taught in the history room	Additional comments
1		
2		
3		
4		
5		

25. Please indicate in the table on the next page the text books issued for the year:

Year	Textbooks used	Qualities	Use of textbooks		
		If you find the following satisfactory please tick: Pictures, Maps, Diagrams, Facts, Narrative	For test questions (Frequently, Occasionally, Never)	In class (Frequently, Occasionally, Never)	For homework (Frequently, Occasionally, Never)
1					
2					
3					
4					
5					

26. Please either enclose a copy of your syllabus for the lower school or complete the following table showing in as much detail as the spaces allow the broad periods, topics, lines of development you cover in the first four years.

Year	Christmas term	Easter term	Summer term
1			
2			
3			
4			

27. The teaching of a topic in history often embraces many aspects of the subject. Please indicate on the table below and on the next page how much importance should be given to these aspects in the lower school by ticking in the appropriate columns.

		1st year				
		Very important	*Important*	*Moderately important*	*Unimportant*	*Should not be taught*
Social	Customs Pastimes Dress Living conditions					
Religion	Ideas/beliefs Story of religion in Britain Story of religion in Europe Religions of the world					
Cultural/ artistic	Music Painting Architecture Literature Sculpture					

Science	Ideas
	Inventions

Economic	Agriculture
	Industry
	Transport
	Trade overseas
	Trade at home

Political	Growth of British constitutition
	Government in Britain
	Government elsewhere
	International diplomacy

Military	Battles/strategy
	Development of weapons

Expansion of Europe	Europe and outside world:
	Ideas: culture
	Colonization

Biography	Adventurous deeds in warfare, exploration
	Problems, difficulties of kings, statesmen
	Other great figures of past

Historiography

Local history

Original sources

Historical methodology

Columns for 2nd, 3rd, 4th and 5th years are identical to 1st year column

28. The following table deals with four topics you may well teach in the lower school. For each year and topic, and for the fifth year, please indicate the methods of presentation and activities you use, showing, by ticking in the appropriate columns, the degree of importance you give to each. Please indicate by writing across the five columns where any of these methods and activities are pursued outside the classroom (e.g. in the history club).

Number of lessons on each topic:

	1st year Norman England 1066–1087						2nd year Voyages of Discovery (15 and 16)				
		Very important	*Important*	*Moderately important*	*Unimportant*	*Should not be done*	1	2	3	4	5
Methods	Exposition										
	Questioning										
	Poetry										
	Diagrams/date/charts										
	Maps										
	Duplicated notes										
	Dictated/copied notes										
	Documents										
	Photos historical material										
	Films filmstrips										
	Historical plays										
	B.B.C. schools broadcast										
Activities	Memorising facts										
	Memorising causes										
	Reading text books										
	Reading historical novels										
	Drawing maps										
	Drawing diagrams										
	Drawing pictures										
	Making own notes										
	Imaginative writing										
	Formal essays										
	Discussion										
	Lecturettes										
	Acting historical plays										
	Field work (e.g. visits)										
	Model making										
	Other project work										

Topic for third year is English Civil Wars; and fourth year, English Industrial Revolution. Fifth year topic left for teachers to fill in.

29. *Practical work*
    Model making
    Individual written projects on a 'patch' or 'line of development'
    Written projects on a local study
    Group projects
    Examining documents and other historical material
    Dramatic work
    Historical visits (including museum)

    The above activities can be defined as 'practical work': the emphasis
    is on the children 'finding out' for themselves. Please indicate your
    opinion of practical work by placing the following possible values in
    rank order.
    ORDER

    .... *a.* To encourage accurate observation and careful recording.

    .... *b.* To promote simple, common-sense methods of thought.

    .... *c.* To develop manipulative skills.

    .... *d.* To give a training in problem solving.

    .... *e.* To introduce an understanding of historical methodology.

    .... *f.* To verify facts and principles already taught.

    .... *g.* To arouse and maintain interest in the subject.

    .... *h.* To make history seem more real through personal ex-
            perience.

    .... *i.* To be an integral part of the process of finding facts by
            investigation and arriving at theories.

    .... *j.* To elucidate the theoretical work so as to aid comprehension.

GENERAL COMMENTS (if any) on the values of practical work.

30. *'O' Level*

    a. What periods are the 'O' level forms covering this year?

    b. Please briefly state the reasons for this choice.

    c. What periods did you cover with the 'O' level forms of 1964 and
    1963?

    d. Are you satisfied with the present form of 'O' level examination?

    COMPLETELY SATISFIED   MODERATELY SATISFIED   DISSATISFIED.

    e What alterations, if any, do you suggest?

f. Do you find that the effects of the 'O' level syllabus on the courses you provide in the lower school are:

Year	Great	Moderate	Insignificant	Immaterial	Good	Bad
1						
2						
3						
4						
5						

g. Assume for the moment that 'O' level does not exist and that all pupils are leaving school at 16. In these circumstances, what changes in *content* and *method* would you make in those forms at present affected?

I would make the following changes (please indicate the year where other than 'O' level): ....

....

31. Please place the following in the order which most nearly represents your aim in teaching history in the lower school. If you have aims which are not included, please rank those given and then add your own in the space below, indicating their position in the rank order.
ORDER

.... *a.* Provide an understanding of how present institutions, attitudes, civilisations etc. have developed.

.... *b.* Develop an attitude of maturity through impartial judgement.

.... *c.* Develop an 'involvement with humanity' through a study of history.

.... *d.* Create a lasting interest in history.

.... *e.* Induce an appreciation of some of the great events in British history.

.... *f.* Provide a framework of facts on which the pupil can later build.

.... *g.* Provide a training in the recognition of cause and effect in human problems.

.... *h.* Provide standards of reference by which to criticise our own age.

.... *i.* Enable children to experience the wonder and enjoyment of reconstructing the past.

.... *j.* Enable children to pass the 'O' level examination.

....

....

....

32. What do you hope you have achieved by the beginning of the fourth year (i.e. before the 'O' level syllabus is started)?

136

Appendix II

Pupils' questionnaire

Name ....

School ....

Form ....

Age ....years..................................months..................

Please write all your answers on the questionnaire paper.

1. What period(s) are you covering for 'O' level history?

2. What topics covered *this year* in history have you enjoyed?

3. Briefly explain why you enjoyed them.

4. What topics covered this year have you disliked?

5. Briefly explain why you disliked them.

6. Did you enjoy the history you learned in your first three years at grammar school more than the 'O' level course?

   YES/NO/INDIFFERENT

7. Briefly explain your answer to No. 6.

8. Here is a list of some of the topics you may have covered in your first three years at grammar school. Underline the ones you enjoyed.

   Early man
   Egyptian civilisation
   Greek civilisation
   Roman civilisation
   Anglo-Saxons
   Norman Conquest of England
   Norman architecture—churches and castles

137

The crusades
Hundred Years War
Voyages of Discovery
The Renaissance
Luther and the Continental Reformation
Reformation in England
Tudor architecture
Elizabethan England
English civil war
Pepys's London
Louis XIV's France
Glorious Revolution of 1688
Agricultural revolution
Industrial revolution
Jacobite rebellions
Methodist movement
British Empire: Canada and India
British Empire: America and the war for independence
Cook and Australia
French revolution
Napoleonic wars

9. Which topic covered in history in grammar school have you enjoyed most? Either choose one from the previous question or select one outside the list if your choice is not there.

10. Briefly explain your choice in No. 9.

11. Do you enjoy spending time on one topic in history, covering it in detail and studying it in depth?   YES/NO/INDIFFERENT

12. Briefly explain your answer to No. 11.

13. Here is a list of some of the activities you may have pursued in class or history club when learning history in your first three years at grammar school. For each activity, decide whether or not you enjoyed it, and whether or not you found it useful and helpful in learning the history. (For example, you may have found discussion in class enjoyable but felt you learned little.) Tick in the appropriate columns. Give some idea of the frequency with which you undertook these activities. Add any other history activities not included which you pursued and mark in the same way. For those activities which you did *not* pursue tick the far right hand column ('NEVER') *only*.

Activities	Interest					Use					Frequency			
	Very enjoyable	Enjoyable	Indifferent	Dislike	Strongly dislike	Very helpful	Helpful	Indifferent	Unhelpful	Very unhelpful	1 + per week	1 + per month	1 + per term	Never
Learning facts (dates/names)														
Learning generalisations														
Reading text books														
Listening to the class teacher														
Making own notes														
Taking dictated or copied notes														
Making date and time charts														
Drawing maps and diagrams														
Writing formal essays														
Writing imaginative essays														
Looking at historical films														
Looking at historical filmstrips														
Class discussion														
Class debates														
Giving brief talks in class														
Examining historical documents														
Examining reproductions of pictures														
Examining photos of historical material														
Local historical studies														
Written projects														

14. Do you think it is important for a long period of history to be covered in your lessons, so that you get a sense of time and distance?

YES/NO/DON'T KNOW.

15. Briefly explain your answer to No. 14.

16. Do you think that the history of our own times (e.g. 1918–1966) is more important than distant history? YES/NO/DON'T KNOW.

17. Briefly explain your answer to No. 16.

18. Do you think that world history rather than national history should be taught? YES/NO/DON'T KNOW

19. Briefly explain your answer to No. 18.

20. Do you intend to study history as a main subject in the sixth form?

YES/NO/DON'T KNOW.

21. What subjects do you want to study in the sixth form?

22. What do you consider your 'best' subject? ....

23. What do you consider your 'worst' subject? ....

24. Do you want to go on to university or college after you have left school? YES/NO/UNCERTAIN.

25. What career to you think you would like to pursue once you have finished your formal education?

26. Do you ever borrow history books, historical novels or biographies from the school or public libraries?

FREQUENTLY/SOMETIMES/VERY OCCASIONALLY/NEVER.

27. If you do read history books, historical novels or biographies, name two read in the last two years you have enjoyed.

28. Briefly explain why you enjoyed them.

29. Apart from school organised expeditions, do you ever go to visit museums or places of historical interest?

FREQUENTLY/SOMETIMES/VERY OCCASIONALLY/NEVER.

30. What are your hobbies or pastimes?

31. Which of the following four statements most nearly conform to your view of history? Put ticks (one or more) in the boxes on the right against your choices.

  a. To learn history is a waste of time, since the past is over and done with.

b. History is an important subject since it helps us to understand the world in which we live. ☐

c. Most history lessons bore me. ☐

d. I enjoy learning history. ☐

32. What kind of historical facts do you remember most easily?

33. What kind of historical facts do you find hard to remember?

34. The facts of history (e.g. names, dates) are easily forgotten. Briefly say whether you think you have gained anything more lasting from a study of history so far.

Appendix III

The pupils

Research sample: numbers and ages (March 31st 1966)

School		Number	Age range
Benborough	B	14	14:8 – 15:5
Benborough	G	20	14:0 – 15:6
Daymer	G	26	14:3 – 15:5
Fairport	B	33	14:7 – 15:6
Neil	B	20	14:7 – 15:11
Scarcombe	G	34	14:6 – 15:5
Totals etc.		147	14:0 – 15:11

B—Boys   G—Girls

Numbers assessed by research instruments

Research instrument	Number
Manchester general ability test (Senior) 2	144
Questionnaires	137
History test paper I	141
History test paper II	143
History test paper III	142
Interviews	136
Entire series	122

Ranges, means and standard deviations; Manchester general ability test (Senior) 2

School		N	Range	Mean	Standard deviation
Benborough	B	14	120 – 143	134·71	5·64
Benborough	G	19	126 – 140	135·63	3·73
Daymer	G	25	117 – 144	130·84	7·14
Fairport	B	32	114 – 138	126·03	7·13
Neil	B	20	116 – 142	128·80	6·46
Scarcombe	G	34	110 – 136	126·00	7·86
All schools		144	110 – 144	129·38	7·70

Do you intend to study history as a main subject in the sixth form? (Question 20)

School		Yes		No		Uncertain		Totals	
		n	%	n	%	n	%	N	%
Benborough	B	1	8	8	62	4	30	13	100
Benborough	G	2	11	8	42	9	47	19	100
Daymer	G	4	15	14	54	8	31	26	100
Fairport	B	5	18	16	57	7	25	28	100
Neil	B	2	11	10	56	6	33	18	100
Scarcombe	G	3	9	9	27	21	64	33	100
All schools		17	12	65	48	55	40	137	100

Numbers and percentages of pupils wishing to take science subjects in the sixth form.

School		N	Two or more science subjects	
			n	% of N
Benborough	B	13	10	77
Benborough	G	19	5	26
Daymer	G	26	9	35
Fairport	B	28	16	57
Neil	B	18	10	56
Scarcombe	G	33	2	6
All schools		137	52	38

Do you want to go on to university or college after you have left school? (Question 24)

Schools		Yes		No		Uncertain		Totals	
		n	%	n	%	n	%	N	%
Benborough	B	9	70	2	15	2	15	13	100
Benborough	G	9	47	4	21	6	32	19	100
Daymer	G	17	65	3	12	6	23	26	100
Fairport	B	21	75	3	11	4	14	28	100
Neil	B	7	39	2	11	9	50	18	100
Scarcombe	G	18	55	9	27	6	18	33	100
All schools		81	60	23	16	33	24	137	100

Appendix IV

The pupils and history: tables of answers

Did you enjoy the history you learned in your first three years at Grammar School more than the 'O' level course? (Question 6)

Schools		Yes		No		Indifferent		Totals	
		n	%	n	%	n	%	N	%
Benborough	B	7	54	1	8	5	38	13	100
Benborough	G	4	21	4	21	11	58	19	100
Daymer	G	12	46	6	23	8	31	26	100
Fairport	B	15	53	8	29	5	18	28	100
Neil	B	11	61	2	11	5	28	18	100
Scarcombe	G	17	52	6	18	10	30	33	100
All schools		66	48	27	20	44	32	137	100

Do you enjoy spending time on one topic in history, covering it in detail and studying it in depth? (Question 11)

Schools		Yes		No		Indifferent		Totals	
		n	%	n	%	n	%	N	%
Benborough	B	5	39	5	39	3	22	13	100
Benborough	G	9	47	6	32	4	21	19	100
Daymer	G	15	58	1	4	10	38	26	100
Fairport	B	12	43	10	36	6	21	28	100
Neil	B	14	78	3	17	1	5	18	100
Scarcombe	G	14	42	4	12	15	46	33	100
All schools		69	50	29	21	39	29	137	100

Do you think it is important for a long period of history to be covered in your lessons, so that you get a sense of time and distance? (Question 14)

Schools		Yes		No		Indifferent		Totals	
		n	%	n	%	n	%	N	%
Benborough	B	6	46	4	31	3	23	13	100
Benborough	G	5	26	9	48	5	26	19	100
Daymer	G	10	39	5	19	11	42	26	100
Fairport	B	12	43	10	36	6	21	28	100
Neil	B	5	28	7	39	6	33	18	100
Scarcombe	G	7	21	11	33	15	46	33	100
All schools		45	32	46	34	46	34	137	100

Do you think that the history of our own times (e.g. 1918 – 1966) is more important than distant history? (Question 16)

Schools		Yes		No		Don't know		Totals	
		n	%	n	%	n	%	N	%
Benborough	B	7	54	2	16	4	30	13	100
Benborough	G	7	37	11	58	1	5	19	100
Daymer	G	14	54	9	35	3	11	26	100
Fairport	B	19	68	8	29	1	3	28	100
Neil	B	12	67	2	11	4	22	18	100
Scarcombe	G	26	78	1	3	6	19	33	100
All schools		85	62	33	23	19	15	137	100

146

Do you think that world history rather than national history should be taught?
(Question 18)

Schools		Yes		No		Don't know		Totals	
		n	%	n	%	n	%	N	%
Benborough	B	8	62	3	22	2	16	13	100
Benborough	G	6	31	11	58	2	11	19	100
Daymer	G	18	69	6	23	2	8	26	100
Fairport	B	12	43	12	43	4	13	28	100
Neil	B	5	28	8	44	5	28	18	100
Scarcombe	G	24	73	2	6	7	21	33	100
All schools		73	53	42	31	22	16	137	100

*Do you ever borrow history books, historical novels or biographies from the
school or public libraries?* (Question 26)

Schools		Frequently		Sometimes		Very occasionally		Never		Totals	
		n	%	n	%	n	%	n	%	N	%
Benborough	B	0	0	2	15	7	55	4	30	13	100
Benborough	G	3	16	5	26	7	37	4	21	19	100
Daymer	G	5	19	10	39	6	23	5	19	26	100
Fairport	B	2	7	7	25	9	32	10	36	28	100
Neil	B	2	11	5	28	7	39	4	22	18	100
Scarcombe	G	3	9	9	27	13	40	8	24	33	100
All schools		15	11	38	28	49	36	35	25	137	100

Apart from school organised expeditions, do you ever go to visit museums or places of historical interest? (Question 29)

Schools	Frequently		Sometimes		Very occasionally		Never		Totals	
	n	%	n	%	n	%	n	%	N	%
Benborough B	1	8	8	62	3	22	1	8	13	100
Benborough G	1	5	8	42	9	48	1	5	19	100
Daymer G	2	8	13	50	9	34	2	8	26	100
Fairport B	3	11	14	50	9	32	2	7	28	100
Neil B	3	17	5	28	4	22	6	33	18	100
Scarcombe G	3	9	18	55	11	33	1	3	33	100
All schools	13	9	66	48	45	34	13	9	137	100

Which of the following four statements most nearly conform to your view of history?

a. *To learn history is a waste of time, since the past is over and done with.*

b. *History is an important subject since it helps us to understand the world in which we live.*

c. *Most history lessons bore me.*

d. *I enjoy learning history.* (Question 31)

Schools	N	a Waste		b Important		c Bore		d Enjoy	
		n	% of N	n	% of N	n	% of N	n	% of N
Benborough B	13	3	23	9	69	6	46	5	39
Benborough G	19	17	36	8	41	7	36	8	41
Daymer G	26	4	15	13	50	14	54	12	46
Fairport B	28	4	14	16	57	14	50	7	25
Neil B	18	3	17	14	78	5	27	8	44
Scarcombe G	33	1	3	26	78	10	30	17	54
All schools	137	22	16	86	63	56	41	57	42

Appendix V

Question 13: pupils' questionnaire

Overleaf is a list of some of the activities you may have pursued in class or history club when learning history in your first three years at grammar school. For each activity, decide whether or not you enjoyed it, and whether or not you found it useful and helpful in learning the history. (For example, you may have found discussion in class enjoyable but felt you learned little.) Tick in the appropriate columns. Give some idea of the frequency with which you undertook these activities. Add any other history activities not included which you pursued and mark in the same way. For those activities which you did *not* pursue tick the far right hand column ('NEVER') *only*.

Histograms were drawn for the twenty listed activities showing the number of ticks in each column for the five schools expressed as percentages of the total sample. The histograms are given on pages 151-170.

Activities	Interest					Use					Frequency			
	Very enjoyable	Enjoyable	Indifferent	Dislike	Strongly dislike	Very helpful	Helpful	Indifferent	Unhelpful	Very unhelpful	1+ per week	1+ per month	1+ per term	Never
Learning facts (dates/names)														
Learning generalisations														
Reading text books														
Listening to the class teacher														
Making own notes														
Taking dictated or copied notes														
Making date and time charts														
Drawing maps and diagrams														
Writing formal essays														
Writing imaginative essays														
Looking at historical films														
Looking at historical filmstrips														
Class discussion														
Class debates														
Giving brief talks in class														
Examining historical documents														
Examining reproductions of pictures														
Examining photos of historical material														
Local historical studies														
Written projects														

Question 13: pupils' questionnaire
1. Learning facts

(a) Interest

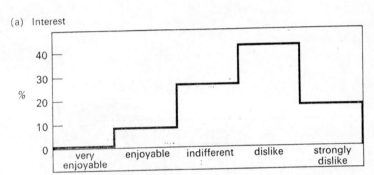

(b) Use

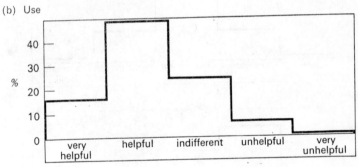

(c) Frequency

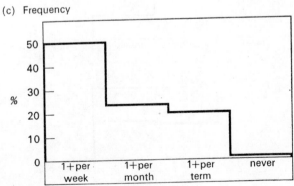

Question 13: pupils' questionnaire continued
2. Learning generalisations

(a) Interest

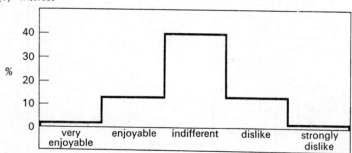

(b) Use

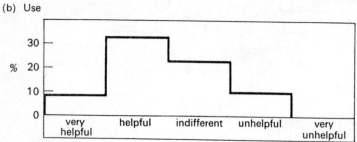

(c) Frequency

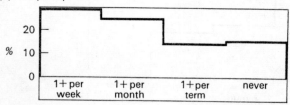

Question 13: pupils' questionnaire continued
3. Reading textbooks

(a) Interest

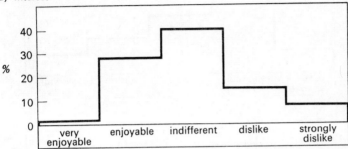

(b) Use

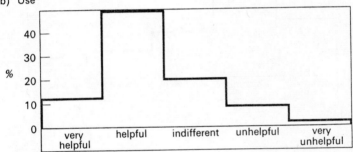

(c) Frequency

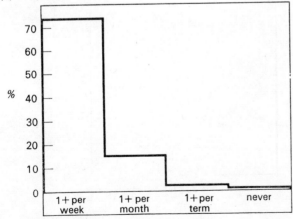

Question 13: pupils' questionnaire continued
4. Listening to the class teacher

(a) Interest

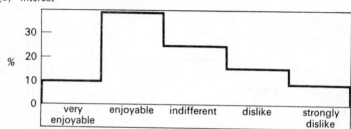

(b) Use

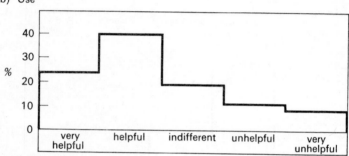

(c) Frequency

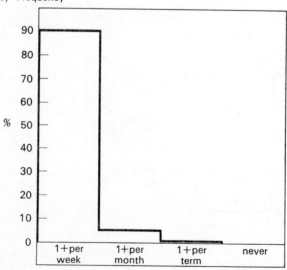

5. Making own notes

(a) Interest

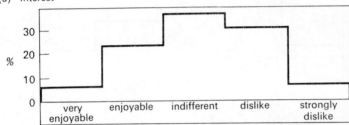

(b) Use

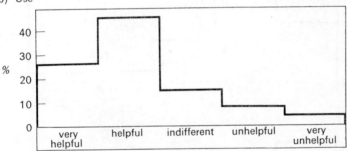

(c) Frequency

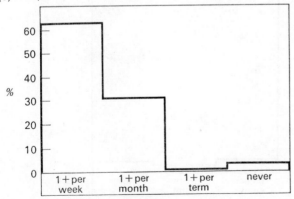

Question 13: pupils' questionnaire continued
6. *Taking dictated or copied notes*

(a) Interest

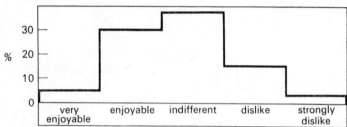

(b) Use

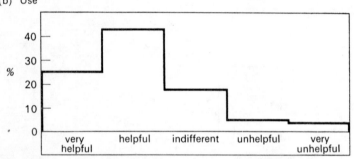

(c) Frequency

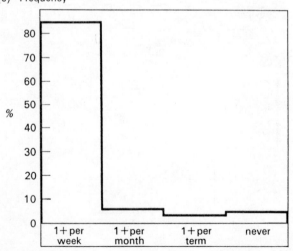

7. *Making date and time charts*

(a) Interest

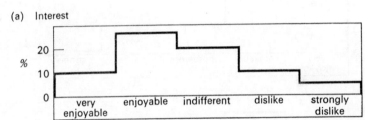

(b) Use

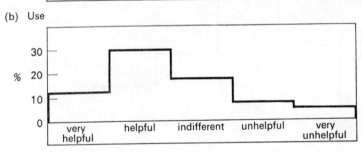

(c) Frequency

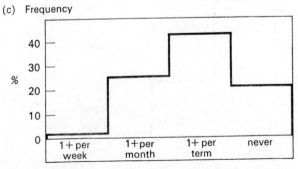

(a) Interest

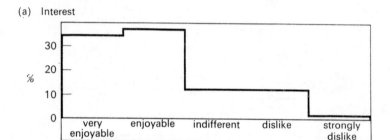

(b) Use

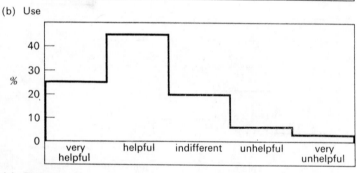

(c) Frequency

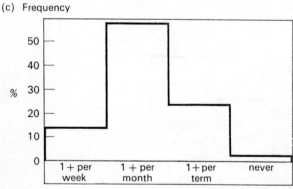

Question 13: pupils' questionnaire continued
9. Writing formal essays

(a) Interest

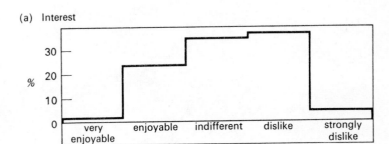

(b) Use

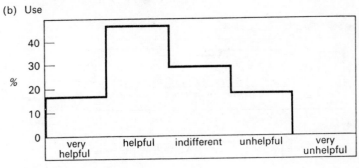

(c) Frequency

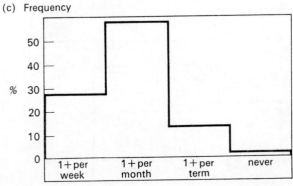

10. Writing imaginative essays

(a) Interest

(b) Use

(c) Frequency

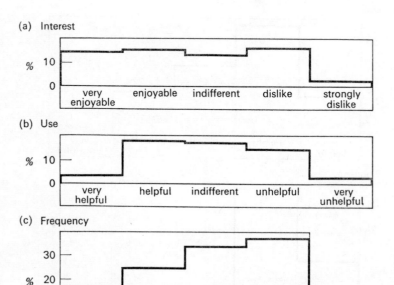

11. Looking at historical films

(a) Interest

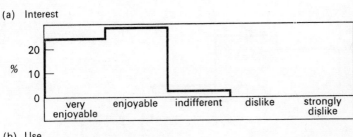

(b) Use

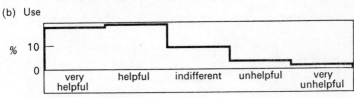

(c) Frequency

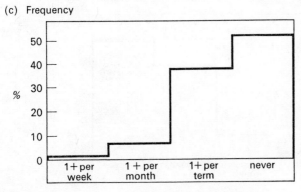

Question 13: pupils' questionnaire continued
12. Looking at historical filmstrips

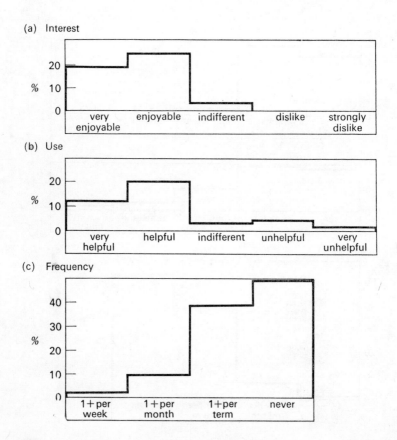

(a) Interest

(b) Use

(c) Frequency

Question 13: pupils' questionnaire continued
13. Class discussion

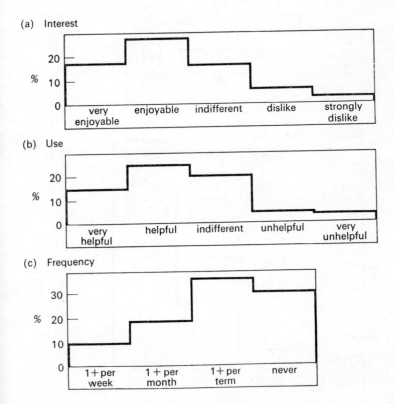

(a) Interest

(b) Use

(c) Frequency

(a) Interest

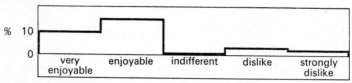

(b) Use

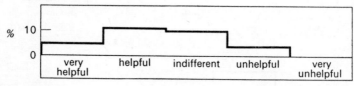

(c) Frequency

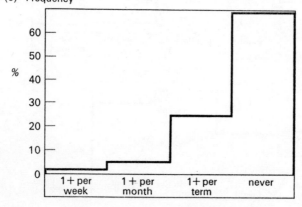

Question 13: pupils' questionnaire continued
15. Giving brief talks in class

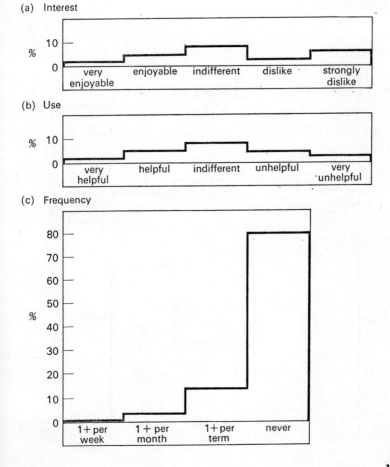

(a) Interest

(b) Use

(c) Frequency

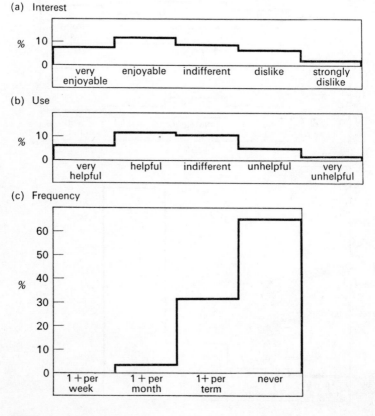

(a) Interest

(b) Use

(c) Frequency

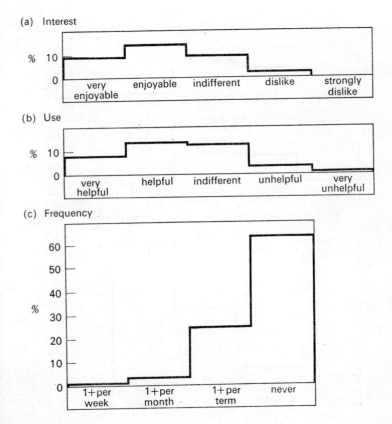

(a) Interest

(b) Use

(c) Frequency

18. Examining photos of historical material

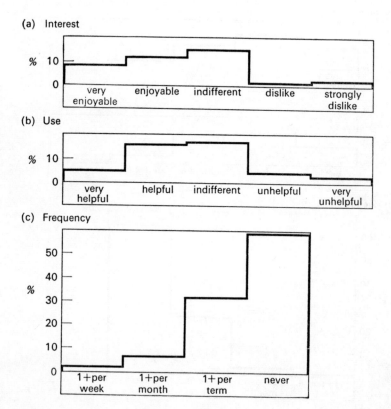

(a) Interest

(b) Use

(c) Frequency

19. Local historical studies

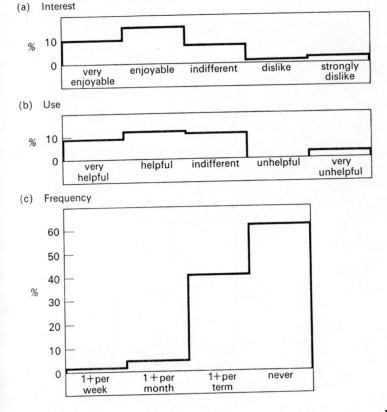

(a) Interest

(b) Use

(c) Frequency

Question 13: pupils' questionnaire continued
20. Written projects

(a) Interest

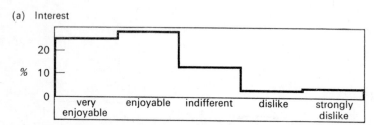

(b) Use

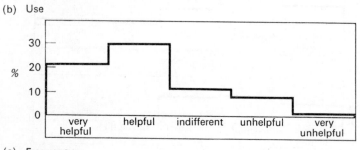

(c) Frequency

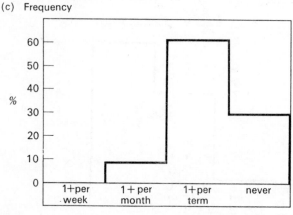

Appendix VI

PAPER I.   40 minutes

Full name: ....Age:.............

School: ....

Instructions

Please use a *pen and ink or a ballpoint pen*. Work quickly and try to answer all the questions.

1. In the lists following, place the events in correct order of time by indicating their positions in the boxes to the left. Against the event which occurred earliest write a ONE, against the event which followed a TWO and so on. The first one in each case has been done for you. Use the space on the right of the page for any rough work you may wish to do.

A.

	American War of Independence.
	Year of your birth.
	Henry VIII of England's break with the Roman Catholic Church.
	Death of Stalin of Russia.
	First Crusade.
	French Revolution.
1	Death of Socrates of Athens.

B.

	Spanish Armada.
	First Labour Party Government in England.
	Dissolution of the English monasteries.
	Assassination of President Kennedy.
	Invention of Watt's steam engine.
1	Discovery of agriculture and the domestication of animals.
	Russian revolution.
	Domesday survey of England.
	Arrival of St Augustine in Kent.
	Napoleon I of France crowned emperor.
	English Parliamentary Civil Wars.
	Viking invasions of Britain.
	Foundation of Oxford and Cambridge Universities.

2. The line drawn below represents 900 years of time – A D 1000 to 1900. On it mark the following points, giving their *approximate positions* and *lettering them*. The events are in their correct order of time. Do *not* give their dates and do *not* use a ruler to measure the distances.

Point A – Norman Conquest of England.
Point B – Signing of the Magna Carta.
Point C – Caxton's printing press set up at Westminster.
Point D – Columbus's voyage to America.
Point E – Start of Luther's attack on the Roman Catholic Church.
Point F – Execution of Charles I of England.
Point G – Deposition of James II of England: the Glorious Revolution
Point H – Execution of Louis XVI of France.
Point I – First English Parliamentary Reform Bill.
Point J – First Petrol driven motor car.

```
   |    |    |    |    |    |    |    |    |    |    |
A D 1000 1100 1200 1300 1400 1500 1600 1700 1800 1900
```

[*In the following questions space allowed in the original papers for reply is not reproduced.*]

3. Suppose you had landed with the Duke of Normandy in England in 1066 and later had been transported by time machine to the year 1750 in England, list below *four* striking changes you might have noticed, for example in the living conditions, the countryside or society. Underline the one change you consider to be most significant and write a sentence explaining your choice.

4. List *three* inventions which you think have influenced or changed society, briefly (in *one* or *two* sentences) explaining your choices.

5. We use the word REVOLUTION to describe:
   (i) the events of 1789–1794 in France;
   (ii) the English industrial developments in the eighteenth and nineteenth centuries.

   What features *common* to both these periods allow us to describe them as revolutions? Answer in *not more than two* sentences.

6. List *two* other events which could be called revolutions, briefly (in *one* or *two* sentences) explaining your choices.

7. The table[1] below shows the periods during which industrialisation has been taking place in six major countries. On the dotted lines to the right of the table fill in the *four* most appropriate countries from the list of five which follows. Two have been entered for you.
   Communist China, Germany, France, Russia, U.S.A.

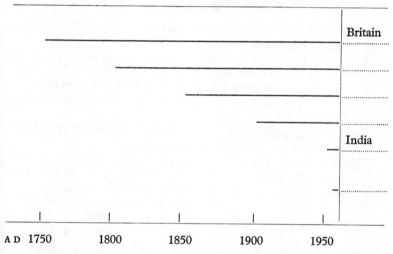

8. Write *two* sentences each giving *one* reason why Britain was the first country in the world to undergo the industrial revolution.

9. The table below gives the approximate populations (in millions) of China, Britain, Russia and the U S A in 1800 and 1960. Look carefully at the figures and then answer the questions which follow.

[1] The table is adapted from one in C. M. Cipolla's *The Economic History of World Population*, Penguin (Pelican), 1964, p. 25.

	1800	1960	Approximate increase over the period
China	perhaps 200	over 700	$3\frac{1}{2}$ ×
Britain	10·5	52	5 ×
Russia	35	225	$6\frac{1}{2}$ ×
U.S.A.	6	183	30 ×

(i) Why do you think that China's population increase is the smallest? Give *one* reason.

(ii) Why do you think the U.S.A.'s population increase is so very much greater than those of the other three? Give *one* reason.

10. Here are *seven* examples of victories won by people or countries of *smaller* population than their opponents. Select by underlining *one* of the examples and give *one* important reason for this people's or country's success.

   a. Normans' conquest of England, 1066–1087.

   b. Puritan settlers' victories over the Pequot Indians of North America in the seventeenth century.

   c. Achievement of Independence from the Spanish Empire by the Dutch in the seventeeth century.

   d. American colonies' victory over England, American War of Independence.

   e. Boers' victory over the Zulus at Blood River, Natal, South Africa, 1838.

   f. Garibaldi's victories in Sicily and Southern Italy, 1860.

   g. Japan's defeat of Russia, 1905.

11. *In 1825* a miner would probably have spent at least 75 per cent of his wages on food for himself and his family.
   Today a miner spends about 30 per cent of his earnings on food.

   (i) Why do you think that such a large proportion was spent on food in 1825? Give *one* reason.

   (ii) On what single item of food do you think a miner of 1825 would probably have spent most money per week?

   (iii) Food is still the largest item of expenditure made by most families in England to-day. What do you think are their next *three* largest recurring items of expenditure over a year?

12. The price of a 4 lb loaf of bread in Britain in 1840 was 10d.

   in 1850 was 7d.
   in 1865 was 8d.
   in 1875 was 7d.
   in 1885 was 6d.
   in 1895 was 5d.

   (i) Write *two* sentences each giving *one* reason for this fall in price.

   (ii) Name *two* income classes of people in Britain who, *in particular*, would have welcomed this fall in price.

   a.. *b*..

   (iii) Name *one* group of people who would have been displeased and briefly explain why.

174

ichard I 'The Lion Heart'

liver Cromwell

olf Hitler

King Richard was English leader of the Crusade of 1190; Oliver Cromwell was prominent in the English Parliament's fight against the King (1642–1648) and later became Lord Protector; and Adolf Hitler was dictator of Germany during the Second World War.

a. Richard I is the only king in the trio. Does this make him the 'odd man out'? What similarities can you see between their positions as leaders and what differences? Write a *short* paragraph (four or five sentences).
b. Each leader felt he had a certain mission to fulfil. For each leader write *one* sentence stating what you think he considered his mission to be.

SECTION TWO

Read the following summaries carefully and look at the photograph; then answer the questions on the next page.

PETERLOO 1819

Background: High prices – high taxes – unemployment following end of Napoleonic War.

Immediate cause: Tory government unsympathetic towards the working class led to a growing demand by this class for an extension of the vote.

Result: Meeting of between 50,000 and 60,000 people in St Peter's Field, Manchester, to hear Henry Hunt, the well known reformer, address them on the subject of parliamentary reform.

Government action: Local magistrates ordered the cavalry to arrest Hunt. The cavalry's charge through the crowd killed eleven people and wounded perhaps 400.

THE GENERAL STRIKE 1926

Background: High taxes – high prices – unemployment following end of 1914–1918 war.

Immediate cause: Decision of the mine owners to reduce miners' wages because of a decrease in the demand for coal following the end of the war.

Result: Miners went on strike, supported by the engineers and railway men. Later all unions followed: in May 1926 the general strike began.

Government action: Mobilisation of troops and volunteers to man railways, etc. At the end of a week the strike collapsed and the unions sent their members back to work. Even the miners, the original strikers, eventually had to give in and accept the terms offered by the mine owners.

[Here was reproduced a photograph captioned: railway strikers at Crewe during the General Strike (a period photograph; the strikers carrying a banner, 'Crewe Labour Party: Workers of the World Unite').]

a. In *one* sentence explain what advantages the workers of 1819 hoped to gain from an 'extension of the vote' and 'parliamentary reform'.

176

b. Look carefully at the crowd and surroundings in the photograph and note down any *two* points which strike you as significant. Underline the *one* you consider to be more important, explaining your choice in *one* sentence.

c. Compare the ways in which the working classes of 1819 and 1926 made their demands felt. Briefly, *in note form*, put down the main differences you can note.

SECTION THREE

[A map of about 1450 was reproduced here with seven areas marked on it, inhabited by seven groups of people, each of which formed a fairly clear, distinct and important social and cultural sphere of influence.]

Seven important social and cultural areas – 1450

a. Name *three* Europeans (e.g. explorers, scientists) who were responsible for extending European knowledge of one or more of these areas. *Underline* the *one* European whom you consider to be the most important of the three you have already chosen and in *one* sentence explain this importance.

b. Choose *two* of the areas and in *two* sentences show the ways in which Europeans dealt with their inhabitants after 1450.

SECTION FOUR

[Four photographs were reproduced, captioned:

A. *Half-timbered houses – sixteenth century.*
   (showing a village street of gabled houses with projecting upper storeys, and small-paned windows)
B. *Stone cottages – late eighteenth century*
   (showing two separate cottages with thatched roofs standing in a well-wooded country lane)
C. *British Iron and Steel Federation houses – 1940*
   (showing semidetached houses on a new housing estate, with steel-frame windows and strips of front garden)
D. *Ribbon development – twentieth century*
   (an aerial photograph showing typical square-junction sprawl; detached houses with small gardens)]

a. What obvious differences can you see in *building methods* between photographs A and C? Write down, in *note form*, *three* of these differences. Give *one* reason in explanation for each change you have noted.

b. Look at photographs B and C and for each photograph *list three point.* (six points in all) you can make about the living conditions or home life of the eighteenth- and twentieth-century occupiers.

c. The street of half-timbered houses is compact; the houses in photograph D straggle along the road.

  (i) What effect would you say this compactness had on the lives of the sixteenth-century people who lived in this town? Give *two* points.

  (ii) How does the sprawl of ribbon development affect the lives of those who live in the houses in photograph D? Give *two* points.

PAPER III. 40 minutes.

SECTION ONE

[Three photographs were reproduced and dated, showing:
  Stonehenge (from the air) – perhaps about 2000 B.C.
  Egypt: Temple of Isis – Third century B.C.
  The nave of Lincoln Cathedral – Thirteenth century A.D.]

a. For each of the three buildings write *one* sentence describing the most distinctive impression it conveys to you.

b. What differences in man's idea of God can you see in these three religious buildings? Write a *short* paragraph (five or six sentences).

SECTION TWO

Roland and his companions have been sent by the emperor Charles to fight the Muslims in Spain. It is the eighth century A.D. Read the following verse below from the 'Song of Roland', a poem which describes the event though written some centuries later, and compare it with the extract on the right from a poem describing the feelings of a poet in the First World War, 1914–1918. Then answer the question below.

A

When Roland sees that battle there must be
Leopard nor lion ne'er grew so fierce as he.
He calls the French, bids Oliver give heed:
'Sir friend and comrade, such words you shall not speak!
When the King gave us the French to serve this need
These twenty thousand he chose to do the deed;
And well he knew not one would flinch or flee.
Men must endure much hardship for their liege,
And bear for him great cold and burning heat,
Suffer sharp wounds and let their bodies bleed.
Smite with your lance and I with my good steel,
My Durendal the Emperor gave to me:
And if I die, who gets it may agree
That he who bore it, a right good knight was he.'

From *Song of Roland* translated by Dorothy L. Sayers

178

B

Bent double, like old beggars under sacks,
Knock-kneed, coughing like hags, we cursed through sludge,
Till on the haunting flares we turned our backs,
And towards our distant rest began to trudge.
Men marched asleep. Many had lost their boots,
But limped on, blood-shod. All went lame, all blind;
Drunk with fatigue; deaf even to the hoots
Of gas shells dropping softly behind.

.   .   .   .

If in some smothering dreams, you too could pace
Behind the wagon that we flung him in,

.   .   .   .

you would not tell with such high zest
To children ardent for some desperate glory,
The Old Lie: Dulce et Decorum est
Pro Patria mori.[1]
(From *The Poems of Wilfred Owen*, edited by Edmund Brunden.)
The two poets feel very differently about the purpose and results of war.
In a short paragraph (five or six sentences) explain this contrast.

SECTION THREE

The following extract is from an account of a tour of England by a German
nobleman who was accompanied by his tutor; the author describes a visit
they paid to London. Beneath it is an extract from an account of a visit to
London, written several centuries later. Read the extracts[2] carefully and
then answer the questions below.

A. We are delighted with London. The city is very large of itself with
extensive suburbs and a fort called the Tower, of beautiful structure....
London Bridge is a wonderful work. The whole is covered on each
side with houses so disposed as to have the appearance of a continuous
street. Upon this is built a tower on whose top the heads of such as
have been executed for high treason are placed upon iron spikes. We
counted thirty. . . .
The wealth of the world is wafted to London by the Thames,
navigable to merchant ships for sixty miles from its mouth to the city.
Its banks are everywhere beautified with fine country seats, woods and
farms. Upon taking the air down the river, the first thing that struck us
was the ship of that noble pirate Sir Francis Drake, in which he is said
to have surrounded the globe. . . .

[1] How sweet and fitting it is to die for one's country!
[2] Passage A from Paul Heutzner's *A Journey into England* is taken from *Elizabethan
England*, ed. E. M. Tenison, privately printed, 1953, vol. 10, *1596 – 98*. Passage B,
from Taine's *Notes on England*, will be found in *They Saw it Happen, 1689 – 1897*,
Blackwell, 1958, pp. 292 – 4. No indication of cuts in the passages used for the
examinations has been made as it was felt this would confuse.

There are theatres where English actors represent almost every day Tragedies and Comedies to very numerous audiences. We visited another place built in the form of a theatre which serves for the baiting of Bulls and Bears. At these spectacles the English are constantly smoking tobacco.

B. Sunday in London in the rain: the shops are shut, the streets almost deserted; the aspect is that of an immense and well-ordered cemetery. The few passers-by under their umbrellas, in the desert of squares and streets, have the look of uneasy spirits who have risen from their graves; it is appalling. The rain is small, compact, pitiless; looking at it one can see no reason why it should not continue to the end of all things; one's feet churn water, there is water everywhere, yellow fog fills the air down to the ground. . . .

From Greenwich, the river is nothing but a street a mile broad and upwards, where ships ascend and descend between two rows of buildings, interminable rows of a dull red, in brick or tiles . . .

Street boys abound - bare footed, dirty. On the stairs leading to the Thames they swarm, more pale faced, more deformed, more repulsive than the scum of Paris. Near them, leaning against the greasy walls or inert on the steps, are men in astounding rags. It is in these localities that families have been discovered with no other bed than a heap of soot.

    a. When approximately do you think the first extract was written? Give your answer as a *date only*.

    b. When approximately do you think the second extract was written? Give your answer as a *date only*.

    c. Do the writers seem to approve of London? Compare their attitudes to the city and explain any differences you may note in a short paragraph (five or six sentences).

SECTION FOUR

George Fox (1624–1691) was the founder of the religious group called the Quakers. Here is an extract from his *Journal*. Read and compare it with the brief account which follows of the recent experiences of an English newspaper reporter in America.[1]

A. After this, on a lecture day, I was moved to go to the steeple-house at Ulverston, where were an abundance of professors, priests and people. I went up to Priest Lampitt, who was blustering on in his preaching and the Lord opened my mouth to speak. The people were quiet, and heard me gladly, until Justice Sawrey incensed them against me and set them on to hale, beat, and bruise me. Suddenly the people were in a rage, and trampled upon me. . . . When I recovered and saw myself lying

---

[1] Passage A from George Fox's *Journal* is from the edition published by Dent, 1924, pp. 72 – 73; Passage B is from W. J. Weatherby, *Breaking the Silence*, Penguin, 1965, p. 19. No indication of the cuts in the passages used for the examinations has been made as it was felt this would confuse.

with the people standing about me, I lay still a little while; and the power of the Lord sprang through me, and the eternal refreshings refreshed me, so that I stood up again in the strengthening power of the Eternal God; and stretching out my arms amongst them, I said with a loud voice, "Strike again . . ."

B. I had read the facts of the lynchings, of the demonstrations, but as yet I was without experience to feel them. At least none of my reading, none of my listening to Negroes in New York, prepared me for my first real experience – of seeing four little Negro girls in their best white dresses walk through a howling, spitting mob for their first day at school in New Orleans. The worst part was the women's faces; the hatred, the viciousness seemed to stand out among the women, perhaps because, being a man, I expected more gentleness from them. It was the next day when trying incompetently to stop a group of white men from beating up a Negro that I earned my first nightmare. They held me and carried on with the beating-up with a baseball bat, and for weeks later I would have a nightmare in which I always awoke trying to scream but making no sound.

  a. Has *English* society become more tolerant since the seventeenth century? Give *two* examples.

  b. Not all toleration is to be encouraged or welcomed. Give *two* examples from *either* English *or* American history where the intolerance of a person or group of people achieved much needed reform or change.

Appendix VII

Extent of agreement between the two markings of the research history test papers.

Analysis of the complete examination over the whole sample (that is, three papers with a maximum of 215 marks taken by 135 candidates) produced a correlation coefficient of 0·923. This figure indicates the extent of agreement between two sets of marks which include the objectively marked items of paper I (see pp. 89 to 92 for details of the questions). However, if the scores for these items are removed from the two sets of marks, the coefficient of correlation is still 0·904. Fuller details of the extent of the agreement between markers are given below.

Marker reliability using total scores on each of the three research history tests.

N	Paper I	N	Paper II	N	Paper III
141	0·907 (0·838)	143	0·845	142	0·932

(In paper I, correlation without objective items in brackets)

Marker reliability using total scores on all three research history tests in each of the five schools.

Benborough		Daymer		Fairport		Neil		Scarcombe	
N	r	N	r	N	r	N	r	N	r
33	0·962 (0·958)	24	0·931 (0·910)	28	0·891 (0·870)	20	0·938 (0·922)	30	0·954 (0·938)

(Correlations without objective items in brackets)

Marker reliability using separate papers in each of the five schools.

School	N	Paper I	N	Paper II	N	Paper III
Benborough	33	0·938 (0·897)	34	0·939	34	0·964
Daymer	24	0·783 (0·743)	26	0·835	25	0·942
Fairport	33	0·863 (0·704)	32	0·813	30	0·928
Neil	20	0·928 (0·889)	20	0·917	20	0·947
Scarcombe	31	0·910 (0·809)	31	0·929	33	0·899

(Correlations without objective items in brackets)

Marker reliability using separate questions over the total sample; research history test paper I*

N	Q3	Q5	Q6	Q8	Q9	Q10	Q11	Q12
141	0·674	0·566	0·731	0·773	0·699	0·636	0·539	0·813

*Q4 was not marked as many of the answers were duplicated in Q6.

Marker reliability using separate sections over the total sample; research history test papers II and III.

	Section 1	Section 2	Section 3	Section 4
Paper II N=143	0·691	0·537	0·923	0·767
Paper III N=142	0·933	0·876	0·924	0·943

Appendix VIII

Extent of agreement between general ability test scores and research history tests, and between research history tests.

Correlations: general ability test with research history tests

	Benborough	Daymer	Fairport	Neil	Scarcombe
	N=28	N=25	N=33	N=20	N=31
Paper I	0·038*	0·218*	0·069*	−0·164*	0·384
Paper II	0·198*	0·203*	−0·023*	0·016*	0·192*
Paper III	0·095*	0·479	−0·336*	0·058*	0·300*

* Not statistically significant

Correlations: research history test paper I with papers II and III

	Benborough	Daymer	Fairport	Neil	Scarcombe
	N=28	N=25	N=33	N=20	N=31
Paper II	0·574	0·367*	0·451	0·435*	0·675
Paper III	0·346*	0·265*	0·354	0·389*	0·421

* Not statistically significant

Correlations: research history test paper II with paper III

	Benborough	Daymer	Fairport	Neil	Scarcombe
	N=28	N=25	N=33	N=20	N=31
Paper III	0·292*	0·431	0·390	0·361*	0·535

* Not statistically significant